MILWAUKEE'S *Italian* HERITAGE

Milwaukee's *Italian* Heritage

Mediterranean Roots in Midwestern Soil

Anthony M. Zignego

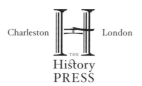

Charleston · London
The History Press

Published by The History Press
Charleston, SC 29403
www.historypress.net

Copyright © 2009 by Anthony M. Zignego
All rights reserved

First published 2009

Manufactured in the United States

ISBN 978.1.59629.836.1

Library of Congress CIP data applied for.

Notice: The information in this book is true and complete to the best of our knowledge. It is offered without guarantee on the part of the author or The History Press. The author and The History Press disclaim all liability in connection with the use of this book.

All rights reserved. No part of this book may be reproduced or transmitted in any form whatsoever without prior written permission from the publisher except in the case of brief quotations embodied in critical articles and reviews.

This book is dedicated to my mom, Cindy, and my Grandma Rita.

Contents

Acknowledgements	9
Introduction	11
1. Challenges in Italy, 1859–1901	17
2. Caught Between Milwaukee and Italy, 1900–1924	37
3. Defining Urban Milwaukee, 1892–1939	53
4. Family Life in Milwaukee's Italian Community	79
5. Cultural Development Amid International Crises, 1899–1945	103
Epilogue	127
Notes	135
Bibliography	153
About the Author	157

Acknowledgements

I would like to thank the efforts and inspirations of many people for this book, and so I shall. Thanks to Professor Michael Gordon for his encouragement and for serving on my thesis committee. Thanks to Professor Amanda Seligman for reading various drafts, for serving on my thesis committee and for being a "historian's historian." A very special thanks goes out to Professor Rachel Buff for her advice on dealing with the complex issues and approaches associated with immigration, for providing thought-provoking questions that inspired further research, for her friendship and for heading my thesis committee.

In addition to my thesis committee, there are many others in the University of Wisconsin–Milwaukee history department who have supported my work. Thanks to Professor Neal Pease for reading several drafts and for his assistance on nineteenth-century European history. The historical methods and questions that I have adopted over the course of my research and writing have been influenced by Professor Joe Austin and Professor David Hoeveler. Finally, much gratitude to Professor Tim Crain of the history department and Jewish studies department for inspiring my passion for history, for his encouragement and for his advice and friendship.

With sincere gratitude, I would like to thank Steve Daily of the Milwaukee County Historical Society for his assistance in locating archival materials on Italians in Milwaukee as well as for his permission to print two documents that appear in this book. Likewise, Shelly Solberg of the Milwaukee Archdiocese Archives was a great help in locating materials, particularly on the early

Acknowledgements

history of Italians in Milwaukee. I would like to thank Ellen Engseth of the UW–Milwaukee Archives for her time and assistance. Thanks to Robert Tanzilo for providing me access to some of his research and for helping me make invaluable contacts. Thanks to Tim Kenney and the Giuseppe Garibaldi Society of Milwaukee for granting access to their photo collections. Finally, much thanks to local historian Mario Carini for assisting me in locating archival materials as well as granting access to the amazing photo collections at the Italian Community Center.

Most of all, I would like to thank my mom, Cindy Zignego, for her continual support of my education through the years. I would also like to thank my Grandma Rita and my mom for their love and support throughout the years. Much thanks also to Katy, who was the inspiration behind the rapid completion of this book during 2009. I look forward to the future with you and hope that our love will continue to grow.

I will personally thank all other family and friends who were not listed here.

Introduction

In 1893 Tom Busalacchi's father paid $52.40 to leave his life as a fisherman in Sant' Elia, Sicily, in search of a better life in the United States. Upon arrival in Milwaukee on June 24, 1893, he worked as a fruit peddler, taught himself to read and became a foreman for a streetcar company. Using this income, he returned to Sant' Elia in 1894 and 1897 to bring his brothers and parents over to the United States. He made his third and final return trip in 1900 after getting married in Italy and arrived in Milwaukee with his wife and his sister to begin their new lives.[1]

Similarly, Jacob Jendusa took out a loan from a landlord in Sicily to raise crops. When a hailstorm wiped out the crops purchased from the loan, Jacob made an agreement with the landlord to pay back the loan. The landlord paid for Jacob's passage to the United States, while his wife and four children remained in Sicily as collateral in the event that Jacob could not repay the loan. In the meantime, Jacob worked as a city sweeper in Milwaukee and was able to pay back his debt. His family joined him in Milwaukee, and Jacob and his wife soon had two more children.[2]

Despite such dramatic and captivating anecdotes, Milwaukee's Italian-American community has attracted an extremely limited amount of attention. Milwaukee is almost always passed over in historical studies on Italian immigrants in favor of cities such as Chicago, New York City and Buffalo. In fact, the only in-depth examination of Milwaukee's Italian-American community is Diane Vecchio's 2006 historical book, *Merchants, Midwives, and Laboring Women: Italian Migrants in Urban America*.[3] The most

Introduction

comprehensive previous examination of Milwaukee's Italian community is Mario Carini's well-researched 1999 non-scholarly book, *Milwaukee's Italians: The Early Years*.[4] This book will attempt to remedy this huge historical gap and create a much more nuanced approach to the Italian immigrant experience by revealing the lives of Italian migrants in Milwaukee as well as Italy.

This book will seek to better explain why people decided to leave their homelands and immigrate to the United States. It is my hope that the reader will find the stories, events and people as fascinating as I do. Furthermore, it is my goal to show what was carried over from other countries and what was either lost or changed to fit into American society. Beyond a better understanding of Italian immigrants in the first half of the twentieth century, this book will hopefully also lead to a better understanding of immigration in the twenty-first century.

To gain a better understanding from the point of view of the immigrants themselves, sources such as oral history accounts, memoirs, newspaper accounts, church records, advertisements, census data and personal letters have been studied. On a broader scale, the importance of political, cultural and economic events in Italy and the United States will be examined, as will their impact on the average person in Milwaukee.

Recently, historians such as Donna Gabaccia and Mark Choate have begun to think about migrations transnationally. In contrast to national histories, "transnationalism is a way of life that connects family, work, and consciousness in more than one national territory. Migration made transnationalism a normal dimension of life for many, perhaps even most, working-class families in Italy in the nineteenth and twentieth centuries."[5]

As she studied the immigration of Sicilians to New York City, Donna Gabaccia noted that beginning in the 1980s, "historians have significantly and provocatively re-interpreted immigrant society and culture. Most recent studies rightly emphasize the continuing importance of Old World values and show how these and New World economic opportunities interacted to create distinctive immigrant families and communities."[6]

Likewise, historian Mark Choate's 2008 work *Emigrant Nation* examines the forces behind Italy's emigration policies, as well as the continuing relevance of Italian expatriates to Italy and also receiving countries.[7] The advantages to utilizing such a framework go far beyond obtaining an international or global perspective.

The experiences of Milwaukee's Italians were very diverse, and there was nothing inevitable or final about the destination and assimilation of these immigrants. Rather, the impact of return migration and a mixture of

Introduction

competing worldviews carried over from Italy and those in the United States helped to shape a unique and varied historical experience, often created and managed by the Italian immigrants themselves.

Italians came from an Italian state in the midst of economic, political and cultural transitions, which resulted in a lack of an "Italian" identity. Instead, Milwaukee's Italians thought of themselves as former residents of a particular town or region in Italy. In conjunction with this regional identity, housing patterns and religious practices were expressions of this regional identity that became reinforced through return migration, or the frequent pattern of making several trips back and forth between a person's new country and his country of origin. As these regional tensions declined after World War I, a broader "Italian" identity formed in Milwaukee, largely along cultural lines, while an "American" identity took shape along political lines. By the end of World War II, many first- and second-generation Italians in Milwaukee considered themselves to be "Americans," yet preserved an ethnic Italian identity.

Chapter one will demonstrate how Italian unification in the 1860s accentuated long-standing regional tensions that were reinforced by political and economic decisions in the new Italian state between 1871 and 1900. On the state level, a combination of failed efforts at instituting an "Italian" identity; the failures to solve the "Southern Question" satisfactorily via emigration to Africa; and corrupt politicians further aggravated the situation. The economic and social hardships in Italy, particularly in the South, convinced many Italians to leave Italy for the Americas beginning in the 1880s, and millions more followed them in the 1890s and the early twentieth century. To make this chapter as clear and interesting as possible, maps have been included for the reader as have humorous political cartoons from the era.

Chapter two will demonstrate that for many Italian migrants, the arrival to American cities such as Milwaukee was not envisioned to be a permanent settlement. Instead, many often returned to their villages in Italy to bring family members and friends with them through "chain migration," while others returned to Italy after serving as seasonal workers in Milwaukee. Other than return migration, Italians remained connected to their hometowns in Italy through relatives, emigrant remittances and international events such as World War I. All of these factors resulted in the creation of a regional identity that was most marked in the period before 1910, gradually weakened over the 1910s and changed dramatically with the United States' 1921 and 1924 anti-immigration legislation.

Introduction

Chapter three will explain what the immigrant experience was like in an industrial urban setting such as Milwaukee. Initially, Italians from southern Italy and Sicily overwhelmingly lived in Milwaukee's Third Ward, while the much less numerous northern and central Italians in Milwaukee settled in Bay View. Due to a variety of forces such as a shift in housing ideals among Italian immigrants, the reduced availability and deteriorated state of housing in the Third Ward and greater economic mobility, Italians began establishing new "ethnic enclaves" such as the First Ward in the 1920s. This process increased during the 1930s as the Great Depression left many unemployed and stuck in deteriorating housing conditions.

Despite the creation of these ethnic enclaves, the Italian community could not have survived in an urban environment in complete isolation. Italians were employed by non-Italians in unskilled labor and, slowly for second-generation Italians, in white-collar jobs. Simultaneously, the Italian community's "regional expatriate units" such as ethnic grocery stores "formed small economic niches and eased the uncertainties of return migration."[8] As early as 1912, the Italian community had meaningful social, intellectual and economic contacts with other ethnic groups in Milwaukee.[9] Some of these contacts would result in the acceptance of Italian cultural celebrations among Milwaukeeans in the 1920s and 1930s that will be discussed in chapter five.

Chapter four will discuss the dynamics of the Italian immigrant family and discuss misconceptions and realities regarding Italian families. Rather than playing a peripheral part as has been typically depicted, Italian women were essential in helping the community overcome the Great Depression, as well as in shaping a broader Italian identity through their familial, social and cultural contributions. This chapter will also explore the impact of return migration on family dynamics within the Italian-American community in Milwaukee.

In contrast to traditional beliefs about Italian immigrants, Italian women often worked outside the home in paid and unpaid roles in Milwaukee. As the second generation of Italians in Milwaukee came of age, the Italian cultural ties were enhanced, while some of the traditional social practices such as dating were weakened in the 1930s and 1940s. In Milwaukee, Italian women took active roles in ethnic businesses, social activities in the community and religious activities that enhanced an Italian cultural presence in the city.

Chapter five will explore the cultural changes within the Italian community, as well as the rise of an Italian cultural identity along with an American political identity. Popular Italian celebrations, known as *feste*, were originally celebrations of an immigrant's hometown in Italy.

Introduction

By the 1920s and 1930s, *feste* became celebrations of being Italian as well as American. In the 1930s, celebrations in the Third Ward were attended by many non-Italians and were replicated in smaller communities such as Waukesha.

In the 1930s, Mussolini's rise to power was a sensitive subject in Milwaukee's Italian community and caused divisions within the Italian community. Once the United States entered World War II, the participation of Milwaukee's Italians via the United States' military service, fundraising efforts and war production further emphasized their American political association. The nature of the war, including the invasion of Sicily in 1943, caused concern for the safety of relatives still in Italy and also led to humanitarian efforts.

The end of World War II in 1945 also marked the end of an almost fifty-year period in which the Italian state had a periodic, yet significant impact on Milwaukee's Italian community. While the political relevance was largely eliminated, the cultural legacy of Milwaukee's Italian community was preserved.

CHAPTER 1

CHALLENGES IN ITALY, 1859–1901

The massive migration of Italians to the Americas became "the largest emigration from any country in recorded world history" as thirteen million Italians left the country between 1880 and 1915.[10] Put another way, Italians composed 10 percent of "international migrations in the century between Waterloo and World War I."[11] While there are many similarities between the Italian emigration and other members of the "New Immigration" leaving southern and eastern Europe by the millions between 1880 and 1920, the Italian migration offers a unique opportunity to link emigration with immigration and its aftermath. For example, an independent Israel, Poland or Ireland did not exist for Jewish, Polish and Irish emigrants leaving Europe in the same way that Italy did by the 1870s. Furthermore, the massive emigration from Italy coincided with the emergence of a newly independent Italy, unlike the German emigration, which happened before unification in that country. Finally, Italy offers a fascinating and unique chance to explore international migrations, since emigration policy was the country's chief international concern until World War I—yet it largely occurred "beyond the state's direct control."[12]

Italian unification took place not as a democratic movement, but as a series of decisions by political elites that did not address the concerns of the Italian people. Despite the emergence of a politically and geographically united Italian state and peninsula by 1871, Italian unification accentuated preexisting regional tensions rather than alleviated them. The resulting sectionalism contributed to economic disparities between northern and southern Italy and was the basis for Italy's state-supported emigration policy.

Italian politicians saw emigration as a vehicle to remedy the regionalism that plagued Italy. Politicians such as Francesco Crispi attempted to use Ethiopia as an emigrant destination, which failed miserably. The chaotic status of southern Italy by the 1890s, along with the failure of state-sponsored immigration to Africa, led to millions of Italians immigrating for the Americas. The Italian government sought to capitalize on this unprecedented migration by reforming its emigration laws and making the migrants "Italians."

Italian Unification

Before the unique and massive Italian emigration in the late nineteenth and early twentieth centuries, Italian unification occurred in a series of complex steps during the 1850s and 1860s, which left the Italian people extremely unsatisfied. The controversies, regional and cultural cleavages and dissatisfaction with the unified state largely can be attributed to Italy's emergence as an independent state by 1871 as the "unplanned product of war, diplomacy, and popular revolution."[13] The unpredictable dynamics of Italian unification occurred because the Italian peninsula was controlled by other European countries, namely Austria-Hungary and France.

The major individuals associated with Italian unification—namely Giuseppe Mazzini, Camillo Benso di Cavour and Giuseppe Garibaldi—had very different ideas of a unified Italy. Mazzini argued for a modern Italy based on democratic principles, but his influence sharply declined after the 1840s and 1850s, since he was seen to be too radical by allies of the monarchy who had little intention of creating a democracy.[14]

In reality, the kingdom of Piedmont-Sardinia was the major driving force behind Italian unification. Also known as the House of Savoy, Piedmont, located in the northwestern portion of the Italian peninsula, saw political stability in the 1850s due to the establishment of a bureaucratic administration, an improving agricultural and industrial economy and the existence of a strong middle class.[15] Its prime minister, Camillo Benso di Cavour, was a political moderate who saw Mazzini and Garibaldi as too revolutionary and instead focused on the economic modernization of

Challenges in Italy, 1859–1901

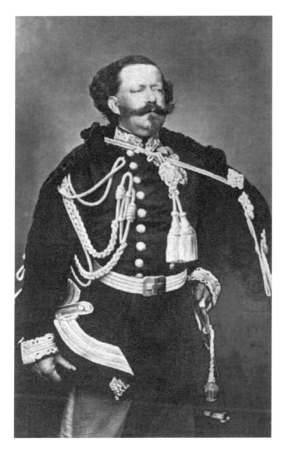

Vittorio Emanuele II, king of Piedmont-Sardinia (1849–61) and king of Italy (1861–78).

Piedmont. By the end of the 1850s under Cavour, Piedmont dramatically expanded its railroad system, increased exports of agricultural products and expanded its industries with help from foreign loans to make Piedmont "the most modern state on the peninsula, serving as a model that all other Italian states attempted to follow."[16]

Though Piedmont's economic modernization and political stability were significant for its preeminent position within Italy, foreign affairs would ultimately make Piedmont the driving force behind Italian unification. Foreign policy politically united King Vittorio Emanuele II of Piedmont-Sardinia with Cavour around the goal of obtaining more territory. After Cavour obtained the support of French leader Napoleon III for a joint French-Piedmontese war against the Austrians drawn up in a secret deal, Austria invaded Piedmont and was defeated by Piedmontese and French forces at Magenta and Solferino in 1859.[17]

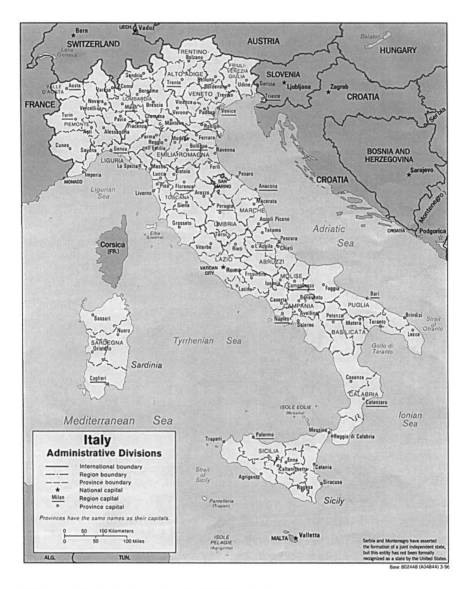

2009 map of Italy, showing regions (in CAPS) and cities.

Challenges in Italy, 1859–1901

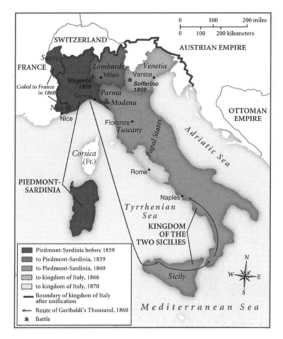

Map showing the progress of Italian unification.

As a result, Piedmont obtained the province of Lombardy in 1859 and in April 1860, Cavour negotiated a deal with Napoleon III to hold special elections in Tuscany and Emilia, both of which voted to join Piedmont, in exchange for formally handing over Nice and Savoy to France.[18] Therefore, Cavour's "ambiguous and opportunistic foreign policy whose principal objective was not so much national unification as the dislodging of Austria from Italy," resulted in a Piedmont that "included Lombardy, Emilia, and Tuscany, the most modern and prosperous regions on the Italian peninsula."[19] Within a few months of Piedmont's dramatic success in consolidating an expanding position within the Italian peninsula, events in southern Italy and, in particular, Sicily made independence a national issue.

While Piedmont provided the main thrust against Austria in the North, the uncertain political state of southern Italy and Sicily created problems that influenced Italian unification and its aftermath. The Kingdom of the Two Sicilies consisted of the island of Sicily as well as the southern provinces of Abruzzo, Basilicata and Calabria and was headed by an Austrian monarch, Ferdinand II.[20] Public opinion became increasingly unhappy with the monarchy, especially after Ferdinand II reconquered Sicily in 1849 and was unable to curtail the influence of bandits in Calabria and western Sicily. The political instability of the monarchy also

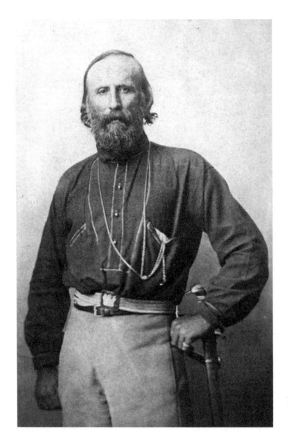

Giuseppe Garibaldi (1807–1882), pictured here in 1861, military leader of Italian unification and national hero.

led to economic problems as Ferdinand II invested vast sums of money on the army and navy while ignoring infrastructure modernization and education in the South.[21]

Dissatisfaction with the monarchy in the South, along with other unforeseen events, connected northern and southern Italy for the first time on unification. In 1859 Ferdinand II died, and his son became unpopular and uncommitted to reforms. In response, Mazzini's supporters attempted a coup d'état in Palermo in April 1860 but failed and were forcibly repressed and executed. In response, the countryside rebelled against the perceived heavy-handedness of the government and Rosolino Piso organized rebels in rural areas. Simultaneously, Francesco Crispi recruited Giuseppe Garibaldi to lead a group of northern volunteers from Genoa to Sicily.[22] Garibaldi and his 1,089 soldiers from the North landed at Marsala, won a battle at Calatafimi against the Austrians and captured Palermo only a few weeks later.[23] Despite assistance from northern Italian volunteers, Garibaldi's success represented a coming showdown between those pushing for Italian unification and those seeking to maintain the monarchy of the North.

Rather than embracing Garibaldi's victories in Sicily, Cavour, "who had never shown any real interest in the South up to this time, was understandably alarmed by developments over which he exercised little control."[24] When Garibaldi invaded the Italian mainland and took Naples in September 1860, Cavour came to the conclusion that "the only way to restore moderate and Piedmontese control was through the unconditional annexation of the ex-Kingdom of the Two Sicilies."[25] To prevent the emergence of the democratic government that Garibaldi preferred, Cavour sent the Piedmontese army into the Papal States where Vittorio Emanuele II led the troops. Rather than engage in a civil war against the king, "Garibaldi handed over all the territory he had conquered to Vittorio Emanuele II in late October" in Rome and Cavour set up plebiscites to be held across Italy justifying their annexation.[26] Once Emanuele assumed control, his general, Nino Baxio, removed the land reforms that Garibaldi had promised southern peasants

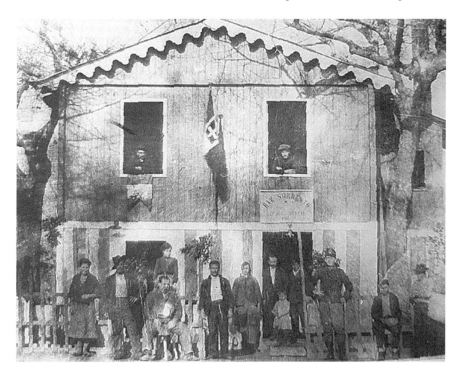

Giovanni B. Zignego (third from right with hands on hips) in Cadimare, near Genoa, shortly before departing with Garibaldi for Sicily.

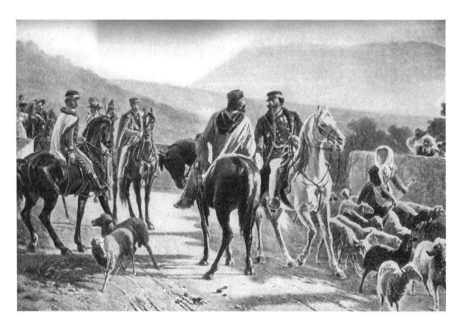

Garibaldi meeting Vittorio Emanuele II outside Rome, 1861.

in exchange for their support.[27] The consolidation of Italy occurred quickly and provided the North with the opportunity to expand its influence across the peninsula.

The unification of Italy came about due to uprisings in the South and expansion in the North. In the territories of the South acquired by Garibaldi, his police forces could not exert control over rural areas and his administration lacked experienced local leaders. Cavour used the political uncertainty in the South to his advantage and argued that Piedmont possessed efficiency and monetary resources, and would grant political autonomy to Sicily. With these themes, admission to Italy under Piedmont passed by huge majorities in the South in 1860. Therefore, some historians have concluded that the "unification of Italy in 1860 must be seen as a strategy to restore Piedmontese domination of the peninsula and as a defeat for Italian democrats."[28]

The immediate aftermath of Italian unification revealed great cleavages within Italy. Following the 1861 creation of the Kingdom of Italy with Vittorio Emanuele as its head, Italy dealt with internal divisions as well as obtaining the Papal States and Rome during the Franco-Prussian War in 1870.[29] Garibaldi's army was disbanded due to its potential threat to Cavour's influence, and and a national draft was established and extremely

Challenges in Italy, 1859–1901

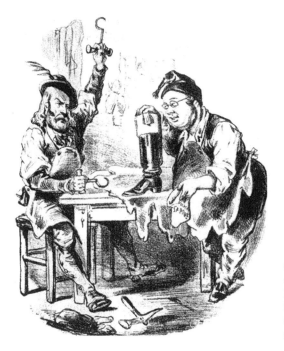

Cartoon depicting Cavour and Garibaldi constructing the new Italian state. Though they have both worked to make the "boot," Cavour is now denying Garibaldi control.

unpopular.[30] One former Garibaldi soldier, Giovanni Zignego, immigrated to Red Wing, Minnesota, along with his nephew John B. Zignego in 1869 and established a farm there.[31] However, this journey was very rare, and most Italians would experience decades of internal chaos until making the decision to emigrate.

An internal "Brigands War" erupted in the 1860s between the new Italian state and southern rebels, which weakened support for the new Italian state and established the notion that the South was backward and crime-ridden.[32] As a result, future industrial modernization was mostly confined to areas that had already begun industrializing prior to the 1870s.[33] In southern Italian towns in the 1860s, peasants either had very little knowledge of unification or resented the new Italian government and sensitive issues such as the *questione meridionde*, or Southern Question.[34]

The unification of Italy occurred in an extremely complex series of events with long-standing consequences. The main supporters of a democratic Italy, Mazzini and Garibaldi, were unhappy with the continuance of the monarchy in Italy. Consequently, rather than creating a common Italian identity, "the unification of Italy actually accentuated the internal conflict between moderates and democrats" and would dominate Italian politics and society in the nineteenth century and beyond.[35]

Italy in the 1870s and 1880s and the Southern Question

Italian sectionalism continued into the 1870s as the Italian state explored ways to go about politically and economically establishing an Italian consensus. However, this proved extremely difficult and controversial as frustration with the South led to the Southern Question, or perceived inferiority of the South in regards to the North. These regional issues were often front and center in the new Italian state.

Southern Italy faced many difficulties before and after Italian unification. There was widespread poverty, high illiteracy rates, high taxation and the Mafia in Sicily—all of which undermined reform efforts to alleviate these problems. Accusations of inferiority often focused on Sicily, which had ineffective police, an almost nonexistent middle class, a shortage of modern agricultural equipment and extremely high taxation rates.[36] Operating under the misassumption that "there was much idle cash in the South," the Italian government increased the South's tax burden by 250 percent between 1860 and 1896.[37] Furthermore, due to a severe shortage of roads and railroads, many southern towns became increasing isolated from one another.[38] The Italian state attempted to remedy these long-standing problems across southern Italy but often was unsuccessful.

The ineffectiveness in dealing with southern Italy was the result of political and social dynamics within Italian politics and society. Following the creation of the Kingdom of Italy in 1861 and its consolidation thereafter, both liberals and conservatives in Italy attempted to quicken Italy's economic and social modernization and were met with resistance from rural Italians and the Catholic Church.[39] Conversely, the future destination of many Italian emigrants, the United States, saw a political compromise after the hotly contested 1876 presidential election. The compromise had significant and long-standing regional implications and resulted in Rutherford B. Hayes's election with the help of Congress, in exchange for the removal of federal troops from the southern United States.[40] In Italy, the political turning point regarding the South also came in 1876 with the election of Agostino Depretis as prime minister. In exchange for the support of southern politicians and local elites within parliament, Depretis granted the South a great deal of autonomy, which slowed many reform efforts.[41] This move has been criticized by historians such as John Davis, who argues, "Southern deputies traded their votes for political favors that strengthened their own standing, but did not oppose measures that diverted resources from the South as a whole to finance public expenditure and infrastructural developments in the North. As a result, the population of the South bore the heaviest burdens of Italy's modernization."[42]

The implications of the continued economic disparities reached far and wide even when reform efforts were made with the intention of assisting both northern and southern Italy. In 1871, 68.8 percent of the population as a whole was illiterate, a rate which declined to only 37.9 percent in 1911. However, even by 1911, 58 percent of Sicilians, 65.3 percent of Basilicatans and 69.6 percent of Calabresans were illiterate.[43] The extreme regional concentration of illiteracy had strong political implications. In 1870 only 2 percent of Italians overall possessed the necessary property to vote.[44] Therefore, there was a push by both liberals and conservatives in Italy to eliminate such voting restrictions. Instead of property requirements, literacy requirements were implemented, making over 2 million Italians eligible to vote.[45] Despite these reforms, the South did not benefit because many southern Italians met neither the property nor literacy requirements to vote.

When attempts were made by impoverished farmers to question the landholding elites in the South, landowners used militias to violently suppress such efforts in rural regions.[46] Southern Italians also dealt with poverty within their local communities. While political support and resources to poor provinces were scant, local clergy members acted as mediators between the rural poor and the outside world. To fulfill this task, local priests often were responsible for the social welfare of the poor and also in charge of a population in which illiteracy was common.[47] However, when the Catholic Church lost its monopoly on education in the late 1870s, the Church's relationship with the Italian government suffered. Local priests became critical of the government.[48] Compounding this problem was the extreme lack of parishes across southern Italy compared to the North.[49] This disparity often carried over to the United States, as American reformers expressed concern over the extreme lack of parishes in cities such as New York, Chicago and New Orleans relative to the ever-increasing numbers of Italians within the country.[50]

In addition to a lack of organization in the South, southern Italians were angered by "the great opulence" of wealth exhibited by cardinals and other members of the Church hierarchy when interacting with local elites. Therefore, in the post-unification years, many southern Italians were unhappy with both the new Italian government as well as the hierarchy of the Catholic Church.⁵¹ The inability of both the Italian government and the Catholic hierarchy to solve the Southern Question eventually led to alternative solutions to deal with widespread poverty, illiteracy and a perceived lack of a common Italian identity.

Emigration: The Solution to Italy's Southern Question?

The regional disparities between the industrializing North and the mostly agricultural South eventually shifted the political focus from domestic policies to emigration in the late 1880s. Italy began to turn to emigration in an attempt to deal with overpopulation, increase domestic wages and increase its foreign influence. While there was great general support for emigration, two very different strategies emerged as to how to achieve this. The first solution was most famously articulated by Francesco Crispi, who argued for the establishment of a "Greater Italy" through the creation of North African colonies, thus restoring Italian greatness through military force like the Romans. The alternative approach argued for the creation of ties preserved between emigrants and their homeland, which would be based on Italy's Renaissance traditions in cities like Venice and Genoa.⁵² Emigration would become a hotly contested debate in the 1880s and set the stage for future Italian emigration policies.

Until the late 1880s, emigration from Italy to North and South America remained relatively low, and there was less emigration from the South and very little from Sicily compared with northern emigration. Seeking better economic opportunities, Italians sold their land and possessions, leaving Europe for countries such as Argentina, Brazil and the United States. To many Italian emigrants, the "United States played a unique role as the most attractive, yet most restrictive country of immigration."⁵³ Typically, northern politicians were supportive of existing emigration policies while southern politicians sought alternative solutions.⁵⁴

The dominant position regarding emigration after 1887 was formulated by Francesco Crispi. Crispi, a Sicilian and former Garibaldi ally, became prime minister in 1887 after Depretis and altered Italy's foreign policy.⁵⁵ The rise of Crispi resulted largely from the defeat and death of 422 Italian soldiers at the hands of Ethiopian forces near Dogali on January 26, 1887.⁵⁶ The fallout from this defeat convinced Crispi that Italy needed to become

Challenges in Italy, 1859–1901

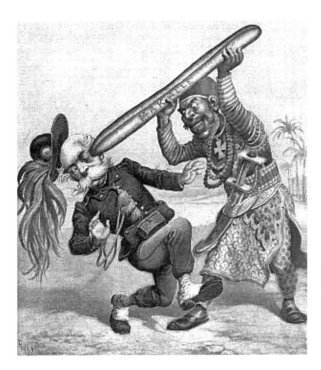

Italy's defeat in Ethiopia was a terrible embarrassment for Crispi. However, it led the Italian state to embrace peaceful emigration as an alternative to colonialism.

more involved in colonial adventures, as the deceased Italian soldiers from Dogali were glorified as martyrs. Crispi also rejected past Italian emigrant destinations such as Argentina and the United States, which were perceived to be "melting pots," and instead preferred that emigrants abroad would become supportive of Italy's imperial expansion through "language, culture, and economic ties."[57] In so doing, Crispi linked emigration with colonialism and as a vehicle to remedy Italian agriculture, making his policies very popular in the South. While supported by some industrialists, Crispi's plans for expansion into North Africa were ridiculed in the North despite his claims that African expansion would place Italy on par with Britain and France.[58] The litmus test for Crispi's Africa plans was another incident in Ethiopia.

Ethiopia had been seen by Crispi as an alternative to southern Italy or the Americas for impoverished Italians. In 1889 Crispi made Ethiopia an Italian protectorate and Italian civilians and soldiers moved there.[59] In 1894–95, allegations surfaced that Crispi had illegally taken money out of Italian banks to finance his partisan newspapers, resulting in monetary depreciation and a recession. Politically weakened by these shocking allegations, Crispi sought ways in which he could transform Italy into a much more autocratic state instead of a parliamentary democracy.[60]

In December 1895, over 200,000 Ethiopian troops killed thousands of members of tribal allies of the Italians, the Eritreans. In response, the incompetent Crispi foolishly ordered the Italian army to counterattack despite being outnumbered six to one. On March 1, 1896, Italian forces attacked the Ethiopians and in a single day, between 4,600 and 5,000 Italian soldiers were killed at the Battle of Adwa, including 268 Italian officers and 2 generals, along with 1,700 Eritrean soldiers.[61] This amazing defeat was "the worst disaster ever inflicted on a colonial power in Africa" and sent the Italian government into chaos.[62] The shocking disaster in Adwa was seen as a complete failure of Crispi's colonial policies and there was a huge uproar within Italy regarding where to place blame for the disaster. Crispi resigned after bringing "the Italian state to near collapse" and other solutions promoting peaceful emigration rapidly gained support.[63]

Crispi's Ethiopian disaster along with economic conditions within Italy shifted attention toward emigration. The economic situation in Italy played a prominent role in the daily lives and communities of most Italians and was often the major reason Italians decided to immigrate to the Americas more rapidly in the 1890s.

A Tale of Two Countries

In northern cities such as Milan, Genoa and Turin, Italy's economic modernization was seen as a positive as new power plants, steel companies, banks and shipbuilding companies emerged in the late 1880s and accelerated in the 1890s. However, the South did not experience the same level of industrial expansion as evidenced by the fact that 40 percent of Italians were still active in agriculture by 1900.[64] Despite the industrialization of Italy, huge portions of the South maintained a distinctive rural atmosphere. In 1896 a Catholic priest named Father Buschart of Milwaukee visited Europe, including Naples, Italy, and reported on what he observed. According to Buschart in 1896:

> *Naples is a queer city and the Neapolitans and their customs are worthy of the stories that travelers tell of them. The purity of the milk delivered to the Neapolitans can be guaranteed as the cows are driven around the streets and milked at each customer's residence. With the same purpose in view whole*

droves of goats are driven about, stopping from house to house. Some of the goats, who have not lost their cliff climbing proclivities, are accommodating enough to climb to the third and fourth floors of flats. The streets of Naples are extremely narrow and filth is awful to behold, yet the gay and the lively Neapolitan, happy in his surroundings, enjoys life. [65]

The industrial disparities were not the only reason that Italians began to seriously consider alternatives to living in Italy.

There was general dissatisfaction with both the North and local representatives in the South. As previously noted, corruption within southern Italy was problematic as "most southern deputies in Parliament supported whatever ministry was in power, in exchange for legal and illegal aid in their reelections and protection from uncomfortable social reforms."[66] Organizations such as the *Camorra* of Naples and the *Mafia* of Sicily often had vast control of urban economies, and "their presence was a barrier to the development of more independent forms of social or political organization."[67] While not prevalent everywhere in the South, the *Mafia* and *Camorra* were among the "most visible indicators of a social ethos that southerners shared," which privileged "patron-client" relations outside of the state's control.[68] The corruption of Southern politicians, along with organized crime, would lead to dissenting voices against them.

Sicily proved to be the location of great unrest within southern Italy. Just as a revolt in Sicily helped spark Garibaldi's invasion in 1860 and led to Italian unification, so too would a revolt against landowners prove to be the catalyst for Italian emigration. Throughout the nineteenth century, Sicily was undergoing the transfer of formerly public agricultural lands and fields such as those maintained by a local community, to ownership under a single individual. Anger and protest had been common before unification, and in 1893, Sicilian peasants organized as the *Fasci* in a revolt against landowners.[69] In addition to opposing southern landowners, the *Fasci* peasant leagues had declared their support for the emerging Italian Socialist Party (PSI) as an alternative to an Italian state flooded with government debt, illiteracy and substandard southern infrastructure.[70] In response to this movement, the Italian government "mobilized a full scale military occupation of the island" and defeated the *Fasci* movement.[71]

For many Italians, the tumultuous 1890s represented the final straw against what they perceived to be an anti-democratic state. The 1861 plebiscite held by Cavour to unite northern and southern Italy was only open to 2 percent of the population, and only 6 percent of the population was eligible to vote by 1881.[72] Furthermore, the belief that the Italian state was hostile to impoverished citizens was confirmed by the practice of incarcerating 200,000 Italians per year in 1876 from southern unrest. The Italian government also imposed high taxes, encouraged trade practices that destroyed local merchants, had an extremely unpopular military obligation, was hostile to fraternal societies and inexplicably decided to ban all Catholic voters in an almost unanimously Catholic country! Being "unable to vote or to find effective political solutions to economic problems at home, 'Italians-in the making' voted with their feet," and decided to emigrate for the Americas.[73]

Emigration Policy

Immigrating to countries such as Argentina, Brazil and the United States, Italians left northern Italy and Basilicata in the 1870s and then Calabria, Abruzzo, Campania and Sicily in the 1890s.[74] Italian emigrants were drawn to the Americas primarily for economic reasons, as laborers typically earned double or triple the wages they could have expected to receive within Italy.[75] They settled in cities such as Buenos Aires, Argentina, as well as many portions of the industrializing eastern and midwestern portions of the United States, especially New York City. Italian emigrants from Sicily began arriving with more frequency in Milwaukee in 1895, though Italians from other portions of Italy had arrived earlier.[76]

According to Italian Community Center historian Mario Carini, at the urging of labor recruiters in New York City, many Italians intended to settle in California. However, many Italians settled on Milwaukee, due to the high cost of travel to the West Coast as well as Milwaukee's location along bustling rail lines.[77] American labor recruiting agents from Chicago and New York brought many unskilled European immigrants, including Italians, to Milwaukee in the 1880s to work as railroad laborers in Wisconsin.[78] Though Mariano Catalano became the first Sicilian to settle in Milwaukee's Third Ward after emigrating in 1884, the majority of Milwaukee's Italians from Sicily arrived in the Third Ward following the depression and agricultural unrest that afflicted Sicily in 1893.[79] Exemplifying this migration, Anthony Machi's father arrived in Milwaukee from Sicily in 1894 with other family members for economic reasons "plus the fact many of his people from the village he came from came to Milwaukee." [80]

Challenges in Italy, 1859–1901

By 1900 about 75 percent of Milwaukee's Italians worked in heavy industries at companies such as Allis-Chalmers, Falk Manufacturing and the Rolling Mills of Bay View.[81] By the time Italians began arriving by the thousands in the 1890s, Milwaukee was home to thousands of German, Polish and Irish descendants "as immigrants and their children made up an astonishing 86.4%" of Milwaukee's population.[82]

Italian immigration to the New World evolved into a mass exodus involving millions of people, and Italian emigrants themselves were the impetus to changes in emigration policies on both sides of the Atlantic. The emigration policies pursued by Italians had a dramatically different focus than Crispi's earlier imperialistic plans and instead focused on Italian cultural and, occasionally, economic ties to Italy. Lacking a coherent national Italian identity due to its recent emergence as a country, Italy made efforts in the 1870s and 1880s to create national heroes out of Garibaldi and Vittorio Emanuele by emphasizing their collaborations and appeal to all classes of Italians. However, such efforts at instilling Italian nationalism failed because of the limited access to public education, and such sentiment was centered in urban areas and thus excluded the majority of Italy, which remained largely rural.[83] Combined with Italy's disasters in Africa, new expressions of culture were sought out as were solutions to increasing emigration from Italy.

Before important changes in Italy's emigration policies, there were those within Italy who were uncomfortable with immigration to the Americas, especially the United States. In addition to preferring immigration to North Africa over the Americas, Crispi feared the loss of Italian expatriates to assimilation. This opposition increased among Italian politicians and portions of the public due to the lynching of eleven Italians in New Orleans in 1891 and three more in Walsenburg, Colorado, in 1895.[84] Italian nationalists also opposed immigration to the Americas on cultural grounds as schools in the United States cracked down on German and Italian language schools and instituted the Pledge of Allegiance in 1893, since these schools were believed to prevent assimilation.[85] Despite these arguments, the attraction of the Americas proved too great for many Italians, and the Italian disasters in Africa discredited Crispi.

As emigration from Italy increased in the 1890s, the Italian government decided to capitalize on expatriates and expanded Italian influence around the globe. In 1899 Turin professor of economics Luigi Einaudi wrote *A Merchant Prince*, in which he argued that Italians should replicate British and German efforts at seeking foreign markets. However, Einaudi's twist was that Italy should do this through peaceful but proactive means by supporting

Italian expatriates abroad rather than traditional European colonialism. As a contrast to derogatory depictions of Italian emigrants, Einaudi cited the case of an Italian emigrant who successfully managed business endeavors in Brazil and Argentina in the 1880s. Einaudi likened this entrepreneur to a Renaissance merchant and as "the living incarnation of the intellectual and organizational qualities destined to transform today's 'Little Italy' into a future 'greater Italy,' peacefully expanding its name and glorious progeny in a continent more vast than the ancient Roman Empire." Such rhetoric "captured the imagination and enthusiasm" of Italians and attracted support for Italy's emigration reforms at the turn of the century.[86]

Einaudi's provocative yet vague notions of "Italianita" were formally articulated into Italy's 1901 Emigration Law. Passed on January 31, 1901, the Emigration Law dramatically made the Italian state more involved in emigration. This law shifted responsibility for emigrants to the Foreign Ministry, which created an "independent emigration commissariat" that sought to protect Italian emigrants from fraud. This commissariat also inspected ports, set limits on what third-class passengers could be charged, established hygiene requirements aboard ships and financed itself through a tax increase on both steamer companies and passengers.[87]

The hope of the Italian government was that the "emigrants would be united through culture, religion, and economics…in a consciously created, global community of Italians under the umbrella of the Italian state."[88] The Italian government also established the Banco di Napoli in 1901, which was a nonprofit organization based in New York City through which seventy corresponding banks in the United States, South America, Europe and Africa allowed emigrants to transfer money "to Italy safely and reliably at reduced rates."[89] The 1901 changes to Italy's emigration policies raised the stakes for Italy and would wield considerable impact, though not always in the ways in which its creators had hoped.

Conclusion

The unification of Italy during the 1860s did not create regional tensions within Italy; however, it did severely accentuate them. As northern Italy became industrialized, southern Italy remained overwhelmingly agricultural and did not receive the same level of investment in its infrastructure and other reforms that the North did. As a result of this disparity, the notion of a Southern Question emerged and initially led to colonization attempts in Africa by politicians such as Prime Minister Francesco Crispi. By the start of the twentieth century, Italy looked to emigration as a solution to overpopulation, illiteracy and poverty.

Italy's innovative support of emigration through both state institutions, as well as cooperation with private companies such as the Banco di Napoli and steamship companies, allowed migration to extend "the limits of the imagined Italian nation."[90] Though largely satisfied with their efforts, Italians' occasional frustrations with "emigrant colonialism" can be explained by the fact that the Americas, particularly the United States, were viewed as "an imagined economic site rather than a place with its own traditions, culture, and history."[91] The very nature of Italy's decision to purse a Greater Italy abroad based predominantly on culture was slippery and put Italian emigrants and their children in charge of decisions regarding their relationship with Italy and Italian culture. These emigrants would become unique, decisive and influential articulators of all things Italian in the New World.

CHAPTER 2

Caught Between Milwaukee and Italy, 1900–1924

In March 1889, thirty-five-year-old Gaetano Balistreri, along with Vincenzo Catalano and his cousin Joseph Alioto, paid twenty dollars each to make the journey from the fishing village of Sant' Elia, Sicily, to Ellis Island's precursor in New York, Castle Gardens. Upon arrival in Milwaukee, Gaetano lived with the Catalano family in Milwaukee's Third Ward, and he made fourteen return trips between Milwaukee and Sant' Elia! After Gaetano and his eldest son Antonio, whom he brought over in an 1896 trip, had saved enough money peddling fruit in Milwaukee, they were able to pay for the rest of the family to come to Milwaukee.[92]

As emigrants left Italy for the United States, they maintained ties with Italy economically, culturally and socially. Many Italians returned to Italy in order to bring other family members and friends to North America with them through chain migration, enabled by Italy's emigration policies. As Milwaukee became a destination in the Italian diaspora, immigrants had to make changes to have a working comprehension of what it meant to be Italian or American. This was further complicated by the fact that this took place during a period of frequent Italian return migration—or the frequent pattern of making several trips back and forth between a person's new country and their country of origin—which reinforced a regional identity rather than a national one. The responses of Italian expatriates, or former residents, to international issues involving both the United States and Italy between 1900 and 1924 shows the interconnectedness of events in Italy and in the United States to Italians and non-Italians alike in Milwaukee.

One of the major distinguishing features of the Italian community was its transience, caused by frequent return migration and emigrant remittances, or the transfer of funds to a person's native country. The exact way in which return migration worked was not well understood at the time and caused resentment in both the United States and Italy. Despite its central importance, this chapter will be the first in the history of Milwaukee's Italians to explore the impact of transnationalism and return migration using primary and scholarly sources.[93] After World War I, anti-immigration sentiment directed against the "New Immigrants" resulted in a series of anti-immigration laws being passed in the United States that, by 1924, essentially put a halt to mass immigration to the United States from everywhere besides a select few countries in northern Europe.

Regionalism's Impact in Milwaukee

As with other cities in the Midwest and East Coast, Milwaukee attracted increasing numbers of Italian immigrants at the turn of the twentieth century. While Michael Biagi of Tuscany was most likely the first Italian to settle in Milwaukee, increasing numbers of Italians arrived in the 1870s and 1880s from northern and central Italy. In the 1890s, southern Italians dramatically increased Milwaukee's Italian population so much that by 1900 there were 1,740 Italians within Milwaukee.[94]

Initially, some of the long-standing regional tensions between northern and southern Italians created sharp divisions among Italians in Milwaukee. In 1903 Father Joseph Angeletti of Perugia, near Rome, was placed in charge of the Italian mission at 189 Huron Street and was greeted warmly by an enthusiastic congregation upon his arrival in July 1903.[95] However, by October of that year, parishioners such as Salvatore Palise claimed that "almost all of the people who go to church are Sicilians and we want a priest of our own race." After appealing to Catholic officials for a new priest, the parish voted entirely on regional lines as "780 were Sicilians who wanted a new priest, while only 209 came from northern Italy and were satisfied with Father Angeletti."[96]

The fury over Angeletti was made worse by the fact that he and educator Hanno Pestalozzi expected one thousand Italians in Milwaukee to donate one dollar annually to raise funds for an Italian church. When efforts progressed slowly, Pestalozzi and Angeletti complained that Sicilians refused to donate

Caught Between Milwaukee and Italy, 1900–1924

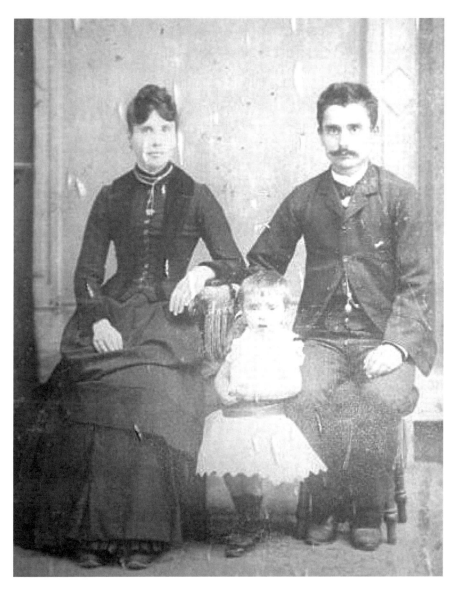

A family in La Spezia, northern Italy, before immigrating to Milwaukee in 1890. In later years, most Italian migrants to Milwaukee came from southern Italy. *Photo courtesy of the Italian Community Center of Milwaukee.*

sufficient amounts. Many in the community did not see an immediate need to establish an Italian church in their new city since many of them had churches in their hometowns in Italy.[97] Such events demonstrate the regional tensions that were translated from Italy to the Italian immigrant community in Milwaukee, as well as the prominent role that return migration would have for Italian immigrants over the next twenty years.

Return Migration

The Italian immigrants shaped their community in Milwaukee on various levels in terms of their relationship with their former country. This dynamic relationship was most evident in return migration, remittances, foreign relations and military service. The relationship between the Italian state and its expatriates was a complex one that sometimes led to tensions, while at other times, exceeded the wildest expectations of both the United States and Italy.

It is difficult to underestimate the dramatic and continuing nature of Italian return migration. Between 1905 and 1920, over 50 percent of the Italians who migrated to the Americas returned to their previous homes in Italy, which led to "many temporary, and changing, diasporas of people with identities and loyalties poorly summed up by the national term, Italian."[98] The interconnectedness of regional identities and return migration further drives home the point that "without the history of return migration, the Italian experience in the United States remains partly unexplained."[99]

Return migration was not a new phenomenon among Italian migrants, as Italians had worked as seasonal workers in other European countries for over one hundred years. Some Italians felt uneasy about leaving Italy, and several Italian migrants from Genoa voluntarily assured an Italian government inspector that they would soon return to Italy after making money in South America.[100] As many Italian migrant men worked as seasonal workers, they contributed to "high rates of return and repeat migration…transnationalism thus became a very familiar even ordinary, way of life for Italy's peasants and workers in the years between 1870 and 1930."[101] Therefore, many of the Italian communities in the United States, such as Milwaukee, had a temporary nature, which will be discussed in more detail in chapter five.

Return migration was mutually beneficial for Italian emigrants and the Italian state. Though supportive of return migration as early as the

Caught Between Milwaukee and Italy, 1900–1924

1880s and 1890s, the Italian state more forcefully encouraged it after the 1901 Emigration Law. To provide incentives for emigrants to return, the Italian government allowed Italian emigrants to maintain their citizenship in Italy and supported remittance banks such as the Banco di Napoli. Return migration along with remittances, it was argued, would benefit the Italian state by promoting economic growth in that country with an influx of funds.[102] Though embraced by Italy, this practice angered some in the United States.

Marion Crawford of the *New York Times* lamented that the average Italian immigrant "leaves Italy, comes to the United States, where he lives almost as cheaply as he did at home, saves all the money he can, and returns to his native land as soon as possible."[103] Such practices led some Americans to conclude that "the Italians come here to accumulate a few hundred dollars" only to "go back home to live comfortably the rest of their days."[104] However, Milwaukee's Italian consul, Angelo Cerminara, argued that the true reason for return migration was the fact that many Italians had been farmers in Italy and were not used to the Wisconsin winters. In order to reduce this backlash, Cerminara firmly stated that "the Italians that are in Milwaukee, one can safely say, are to stay."[105]

Despite Cerminara's assertation, some Italians in Milwaukee still felt much more comfortable in their Italian hometowns. When Gaetano Balistreri needed eye surgery in 1911, "he sold the store to return to Sicily for eye surgery, because he felt that the surgeons in Sicily were better than those in America."[106] The excerpt below from the *Catholic Citizen* in 1906 sheds additional light on the process of return migration:

> *The annual hegira from the Italian colony to Sunny Italy has begun. During November hundreds of Milwaukee Italians have left this city for their old homes. Most of them are single men. They remain in Italy for the winter, and nearly all of them return to this country in the spring. It is estimated that each one of them leaves with about $1,000. And they return with practically the same amount. Most of them are from southern Italy—Palermo and Messina. They spend the winter in Italy, living in ease, and are the envy of their fellow countrymen, and when they return, they usually bring another section of the family with them.*[107]

The practice of not spending large amounts of money within Italy sometimes frustrated Italian authorities and Italian emigrants alike. While many Italians migrated seasonally between Italy and the United States

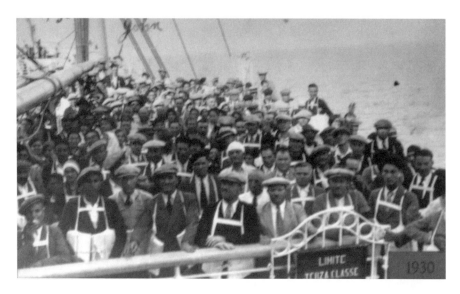

Many Italian migrants traveled cheaply via third class and took advantage of lenient Italian citizenship policies, which made many return trips possible. Notice the high percentage of men. *Photo courtesy of the Italian Community Center of Milwaukee.*

as described above, other Italians always intended to settle back in Italy eventually. However, often when Italians returned from the Americas and attempted to buy land in Italy on which to retire, many landlords branded them as *Americani*, or Americans, and tried charging them exorbitant sums, which convinced those emigrants to return again to North America.[108] While landowners in Italy made it difficult for return migrants to successfully obtain affordable land, increased trade between the United States and Italy made return migration cheap.

In Italian port cities such as Genoa, Palermo and Naples, migrants could obtain passage to New York City and other places in the Americas rather easily.[109] By 1900 competition among shipping companies led to the availability of return tickets to Italian migrants for the equivalent of about two weeks' pay in the United States. These return migrants would often come to the United States in February, return to Italy via Naples in November or December, spend the winter in their Italian hometown and then repeat the process.[110] Return migration became a distinctive feature of Italian migration and was viewed with mixed results in the United States and Italy.

In addition to recurring migrations between the United States and Italy, migrations also took place within the United States. After disease wiped out

Caught Between Milwaukee and Italy, 1900–1924

grape production in northern Italy, Rudy Bertolas's father emigrated from a town near Trento, along with many former agricultural laborers, to New York City in 1912 and the group worked as underground tunnel diggers. When the United States entered World War I in 1917, the demand for iron ore shot up dramatically, as did the demand for labor. In response, "all the people from that area (Trento) moved up to Ironwood, Michigan and worked in the mines up there." By 1923 the demand for iron ore declined, and many of the Trentini friends decided to move to Milwaukee and helped to establish the sewer system.[111] The village-based identity held by Italian migrants was extensive and penetrated not only economic and return migration decisions, but also emigrant remittances that further connected migrants to their homeland.

Remittances, or monetary transfers, became common among Italian emigrants. As previously mentioned, the Banco di Napoli was the main vehicle for Italian remittances and transferred 9.3 million lire in 1903 to Italy and over 84 million lire by 1914. The prevalence of remittances was evident in the United States as Italian-Americans sent $52 million to Italy through 2,625 banks.[112] Before state-sponsored remittance programs, *banchisti*

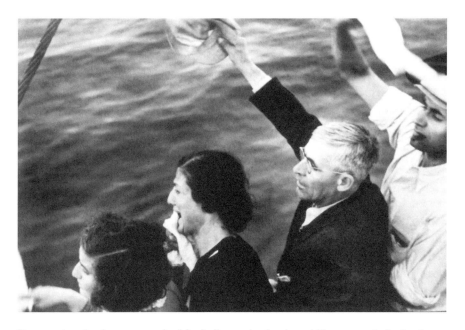

Return migration became standard for Italian males, but it could be traumatic for family members such as Rosa Lalli Camillo (holding hankerchief), pictured here in 1935 Naples.
Photo courtesy of the Italian Community Center of Milwaukee.

handled remittance transactions. *Banchisti* often spoke English and were well respected by Italian immigrants since they were often financially successful, spoke with local American officials when other Italians had trouble and, like *padroni*, were very well respected in the community. *Banchisti* were also connected to return migration as they sold steamship tickets, handled mail from Italy, offered legal assistance and directed Italian immigrants toward available jobs in cities.[113]

After being accredited by Italian banks, the *banchista* would handle immigrants' deposits and send the money from an immigrant to his family in Italy via an Italian bank such as the Banco di Sicilia or the Banco di Napoli. By 1900 there were 2,625 immigrant banks in the United States, including 684 Italian banks "located in 146 cities and serviced a population of 1,328,000 Italians."[114] Once the Italian bank received the funds, the recipient would sign a money order, and the immigrant's family member would receive the funds. The American *banchista* gave the money order's receipt to the American immigrant as proof of transfer.[115]

However, reports of abuses by the *banchisti* through embezzlement along with the desire of the Italian government to capitalize on emigrant remittances led to the stipulation in the 1901 emigration law that each *banchista* had to abide by the American regulation of posting a financial security, and each *banchista* had to have the approval of the Italian government.[116] As an alternative to the existing practices of the *banchisti*, the Banco di Napoli opened branches in American cities and then sent funds to immigrants' families via the Italian postal service.[117]

Once branches opened in American cities, the Banco di Napoli handled 25 percent of emigrant remittances by 1910. While usually more secure than the *banchisti* process, the opening of new branches was expensive in the Americas and was met with resistance by both American and Italian bankers. The transnational dynamic of this process made it difficult for either the American or Italian governments to curtail *banchisti* practices. In 1910 the United States passed a federal Postal Savings Law that made it easier for immigrants to invest safely in American banks. This law was increasingly successful during World War I as American nationalists and some Italian leaders urged immigrants to invest in the United States. While immigration to the United States remained high, return migration sharply dropped after 1911 as Italians started to deposit funds "in American post offices and in time, invested them in real estate or in a family business in the United States."[118]

In Milwaukee, the Italian Mutual Savings Bank was established in 1907 and possessed forty stockholders with offices originally within the Italian

Caught Between Milwaukee and Italy, 1900–1924

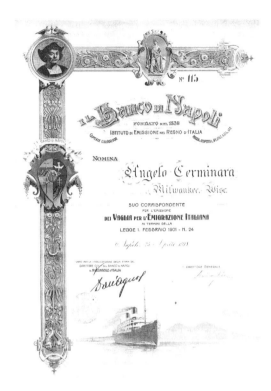

Official charter presented to Angelo Cerminara by the general director of the Banco di Napoli, authorizing the establishment of an immigrant remittance bank in Milwaukee.
Image courtesy of the Milwaukee County Historical Society.

consulate in the city.[119] The Italian bank was owned by stockholders with familiar Milwaukee surnames such as Conti and Maniaci.[120] By 1929 an advertisement for the Columbia Savings Bank located on 418 Jackson Street listed N.S. Maniaci as its treasurer and D.M Guiuli as its president.[121]

While the Columbia Savings Bank promoted its "22 years of distinguished service" and its incorporation date as 1907, it is likely, though uncertain, that this bank was either the Italian Savings Bank referred to in 1907, or had merged with the Italian Savings Bank.[122] Further credence is given to this as Peter Pizzino recalled that "Papa Maniaci" and his partner ran the bank "known as the Little Italy Bank." The bank faced a potentially debilitating situation when Maniaci's partner fled to Italy with a large portion of the money. However, "Maniaci made good on everything owed to the people in the Third Ward and First Ward."[123]

While the Columbia Savings Bank provided Italian immigrants in Milwaukee the chance to invest capital in the United States, the Banco di Napoli authorized the establishment of a branch in Milwaukee through the Italian consul, Angelo Cerminara. Citing the 1901 Italian Emigration Law, the Milwaukee branch of the Banco di Napoli was established on April 25,

1918.[124] While the extent of resources transferred from Milwaukee to Italy via the Banco di Napoli cannot be ascertained due to privacy issues, the development of Italian-owned and -operated banks as both private banks as well as state-affiliated ones demonstrates the strong economic incentives for Milwaukee's Italians to remain connected to Italy prior to 1920.

The impact of emigrant remittances sparked polar conclusions about their impact. While Italians such as Giustino Fortunato of Basilicata, in southern Italy, argued in 1897—before the 1901 emigration reforms—that emigrant remittances arriving in Italy by the millions of lire "save entire provinces of our Mezzogiorno from starvation," other Italians and Americans grew dissatisfied with this practice.[125] Southern Italy received more remittances, yet "mass migration did not raise southern Italy to the prosperity achieved by the North because remittances invested in land and real estate in the South bore fewer returns than money injected into the North's growing economy."[126]

Despite this discrepancy, the *Catholic Citizen* remarked, "Italy has progressed faster in the last ten or fifteen years than any other country in Europe." While not directly connecting the "era of unprecedented prosperity" in Italian manufacturing to emigrant remittances, the Milwaukee paper did note that "the savings banks of Italy are beginning to bulge with deposits." [127] The debate over the impact of remittances led to American opposition and new Italian alternatives. As the twentieth century progressed, debates over the relationship of Italian emigrants with Italy and with the United States intensified in debates over relief efforts, World War I and immigration policy.

A Changing World

Rather than taking a backseat to American and Italian interests, the loyalties of Italian expatriates were fiercely contested when international events arose that involved the United States or Italy. On December 28, 1908, a huge earthquake shook Italy and leveled Messina, Sicily, destroying three hundred towns in southern Italy and killing over 120,000 people.[128] Many Italians in Milwaukee were personally affected by this tragedy, including Italian consul Angelo Cerminara, who traveled to Catanzaro, Italy, days after the earthquake to inquire about his mother, whom sources believed had been killed.[129] In response, many Italian mutual aid societies channeled money to family members in Italy. The Catholic Church in the United States raised thousands of dollars for relief efforts from non-Italians, while Italian-Americans donated funds to their hometowns and remaining family members in Italy.[130] The overwhelming support for devastated Italians from Italian emigrants and non-Italians alike in the United States was unique, as the harmonious goodwill of the international community often did not go beyond non-humanitarian concerns.

Despite the outpouring of support from Italian expatriates following the 1908 earthquake, Italian emigration came to be seen as negative within Italy. Emigration provided Italy with many benefits, such as the cash influx from remittances that fueled industrial development, the creation of new markets in North America and an increased role in international affairs. However, southern Italy experienced a mass exodus as evidenced by the drop in Sicily's population by 108,000 between 1901 and 1911.[131] Furthermore, Italian nationalists argued that emigration was an embarrassment to Italy's international reputation, and Italy should therefore pursue an empire based on nationalism that would help overcome its poverty problems. In 1910–11 Italian novelist Enrico Corradini glorified Crispi's legacy, and nationalists within Italy popularized the idea of obtaining Libya from Turkey through war.[132] In October 1911, Italy invaded Libya, and after several setbacks, Italy obtained Libya from Turkey after spending 1.3 billion lire and using over 100,000 troops.[133] Italy's return to imperialistic policies in Africa marked the first time since Crispi almost twenty years earlier that Italy sought expansion through avenues other than trade and peaceful emigration, angering others in the international community.

One of the major goals of the Libyan War was to unite the expatriate communities. This goal was largely successful as witnessed by the celebration of the end of the conflict "by residents of Milwaukee's Italian colony with a parade."[134] In addition to the parade, Milwaukee resident Frank La Piana praised "the assistance which the American colonies gave the mother country during the war, without which Italy could never have put up the winning fight that she did."[135] Though popular among Italian expatriates, Italy was criticized by a British newspaper in 1911 since "a nation which numbers Calabria and Apulia among its provinces need not go abroad for a civilizing mission. Italy has an Africa at home."[136] Perhaps with this sentiment in mind, at the same celebration in Milwaukee, speaker Hanno Pestalozzi also was careful to emphasize the importance of public schools for Italian children so as to instill "on them the principles of American patriotism."[137] In some ways, the unique position of Milwaukee's Italians during the war between Italy and Turkey would serve as a precursor to their position during World War I.

By 1911 there were six million Italians abroad—equal to almost one-sixth of the Italians residing in Italy.[138] In addition to containing the Italian bank, the Italian consulate office in Milwaukee also served Italians throughout Wisconsin, as well as in Iowa. It represented legal cases in which Italian laborers were killed and was consulted when Italians made real estate purchases. As Angelo Cerminara noted, "The hope of every Italian is that his son or daughter may become a good American and a noble Italian."[139] These dual goals would come under increasing pressure during World War I as interests on both sides of the Atlantic competed for the services of Italians living abroad.

The major issue at stake was the fact that all male Italian citizens, both at home and abroad, were subject to mandatory military service. When Italy entered World War I in May 1915, Italy was the only European country to experience a population increase during the war, due to the return of over 300,000 expatriates, including 103,259 from North America. Despite the large migration to Italy, 500,000 Italians opted not to return to Italy for service since many decided to focus on the country where their children would be raised and feared the loss or non-attainment of United States citizenship.[140]

In Milwaukee, some Italians who had decided not to fight for Italy applied for draft exemptions once the United States entered World War I in 1917. This angered Milwaukeeans such as George H. Russell, who took the position that "as a mere matter of equity, all physically fit single aliens enjoying the protection of the United States must fight for this country in our great war of defense and for humanity, or go back home and fight there."[141] In response, consul Angelo Cerminara informed Milwaukee's Italian citizens seeking exemptions from the Selective Service Act that they must return to Italy or "accept the draft" into the United States Army.[142] Despite Cerminara's position on this issue, the role of the Italian consulate in Milwaukee and the opinion of Milwaukee's Italian population on the war is quite complex, as revealed through the actions of individual members of the community.

Sentiments were split almost right down the middle as evidenced by the fact that 500 Milwaukee Italians enlisted for the United States army while "700 returned to their native country for service."[143] While the exact motivations for joining the Italian or United States militaries may be impossible to discover, the relatively high number of participants in the

Caught Between Milwaukee and Italy, 1900–1924

Italian army from Milwaukee may be attributed to Cerminara's prewar position that likened possible American intervention in Mexico to the lack of protection for Italians in New Orleans, 11 of whom were killed in 1891. While Cerminara advocated legal action on behalf of American citizens against Mexican raids, his comparison with Italian persecution from a Louisiana mob in 1891 to the United States Army may have resonated within the Italian community and caused some to be suspicious of the American military at that time.[144]

Some Italian fraternal organizations, such as the Bay View–based Garibaldi Society, used group finances to purchase $200 worth of American Liberty bonds.[145] From a national perspective, the fact that Italian expatriates purchased 6.5 percent of war bonds in 1917 and 10.6 percent in 1918—and the lack of data on the contributions of Milwaukee's Italian population for either the United States or Italy—should provide caution against definitively identifying the position of Milwaukee's Italians during World War I.[146]

However, some general trends can be gleaned from the position of Milwaukee's Italians during World War I and the 1910s. The participation of some of Milwaukee's Italians in Italy's war effort during World War I overall was not extremely controversial, largely because of the fact that Italy was an ally of the United States during World War I. This is significant since there was no widespread anti-Italian backlash in Milwaukee during or after World War I in Milwaukee, as had been the case with anti-German sentiment and hysteria in Milwaukee during World War I. The anti-German hysteria in Milwaukee resulted in the changing of German surnames, the closing of German stores and the decline of German-language schools.[147] The lack of a backlash targeted specifically against the Italians allowed for the strong continuance of a viable Italian community and culture in Milwaukee well into the 1930s and 1940s. However, the 1910s also witnessed an increase in anti-immigration sentiments both in Milwaukee and across the United States.

American Immigration Policy

Tensions over the place of immigrants in American cities was hotly debated across the United States before World War I and continued thereafter into the 1920s. University of Wisconsin sociology professor E.A. Ross supported the Burnett Immigration Bill being discussed in the United States Congress in 1914, which would impose literacy requirements on potential immigrants.

According to Ross, since most Italian-Americans came from southern Italy, they were often illiterate and tied to organized crime. Therefore, Ross claimed that "as regards Italians, the exclusion of illiterates would be decidedly good for the country."[148] Social scientists such as Ross often differentiated between northern Italians as being worthy of American citizenship while their southern counterparts had "a propensity towards personal violence," lacked teamwork skills and had a "lack of mental ability."[149]

Despite Ross's claims, a 1915 study on Milwaukee's Italian community revealed that rather than being unemployed or affiliated with crime, most Italians were "generally reduced to laboring with shovel and pick in the streets or on the railroads."[150] To refute Ross's position sharply, Angelo Cerminara wrote back that President Woodrow Wilson opposed the literacy requirement and that "neither Prof. Ross, nor those that are defending the literacy test, would ever think of working on the railroads and construction works and on the streets, and the progress of this country would be naturally impeded" should the legislation pass.[151]

However, Wilson also displayed great disdain for New Immigrants and lamented that in contrast to northern Europeans who "added to the vital working force of the country…now there came multitudes of men of the lowest class from the south of Italy and men of the meaner sort of Hungary and Poland, men out of the ranks where there was neither skill nor energy nor any initiative of quick intelligence."[152] Likewise, the U.S. Bureau of Immigration in 1899 divided Italians between acceptable "Keltic" northern Italians and undesirable "Iberic" southern Italians.[153]

Independent of policy makers, similar racial sentiments were expressed by ordinary Americans. In 1914, the popular magazine *World's Work* petitioned the U.S. government to pass exclusionary laws "aimed specifically at the southern Italians, similar to our immigration laws against Asiatics," since southern Italians were unassimable.[154] In Wisconsin, Fred R. Zimmerman joined the Ku Klux Klan in 1922 and became Wisconsin's secretary of state in 1923. Despite publically avowing that he was no longer a Klansman, many New Immigrants, including Italians, were wary of his subsequent election as Wisconsin governor in 1927.[155] The literacy test debate and racial attitudes in the United States foreshadowed more restrictive immigration.

Despite Wilson's veto in 1915 and again in 1917, Congress overrode the veto and the Burnett Bill became law in 1917.[156] Following World War I, isolationist sentiment increased, resulting in the 1921 and 1924 immigration bills, which imposed strict limitations against New Immigrants such as the Italians, resulting in a decrease in Italian immigration to the United States

Caught Between Milwaukee and Italy, 1900–1924

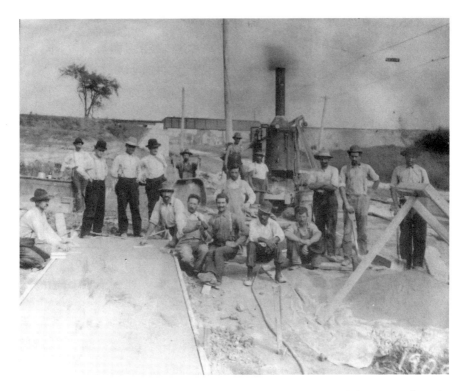

The ready availability of unskilled, manual labor jobs in industry and infrastructure brought many male migrants to growing northern cities like Milwaukee. *Photo courtesy of the Italian Community Center of Milwaukee.*

from 349,042 in 1920 to 29,723 in 1925, all but ending the practice of return migration.[157] With the effective end of immigration from Italy by 1924, Milwaukee's Italian-American community would face the task of establishing an Italian identity with sharply reduced interactions with the Italian government and citizens. Often combining elements of American culture and practices with their own, the Italian-Americans in Milwaukee would become more heterogeneous with subsequent generations.

Conclusion

The relationship between Italian expatriates and Italy was complex and, at various points between 1900 and 1924, frustrated those in the United

States and Italy alike. While northern Italy greatly benefited from emigrant remittances, southern Italy continued to experience difficulties, leading to the 1912 invasion of Libya as an alternative to preexisting emigration practices. In Milwaukee, the practice of return migration seemed peculiar to some, as did the return of Milwaukee's Italians to serve for Italy during World War I. Contentious Italian practices in Milwaukee were often mediated by the Italian consulate, and Italian consuls, such as Angelo Cerminara, often spoke in defense of their fellow Italians. Italian leaders during this era were also often quick to point out the importance of Italians within both Milwaukee and the United States and pressed the Italian population to embrace the American educational system and establish themselves in the United States.

Though the physical ties to Italy were cut off by 1924, Milwaukee's Italians had been integrating cultural ties to Italy since they first began arriving in the city and modifying them within American society. The next chapters will expand the scope of the community beyond consuls and international affairs and focus much more on ordinary citizens.

CHAPTER 3

Defining Urban Milwaukee, 1892–1939

The Italian government was not alone in differentiating between various groups of Italians. By 1899 the U.S. Bureau of Immigration differentiated between acceptable northern Italians and unacceptable southern Italians. Even progressive reformers such as Jane Addams claimed that "South Italians more than any other immigrants, represent the pathetic stupidity of agricultural people crowded into city tenements."[158] With restrictive government immigration laws being passed in the mid-1920s, the regional tensions common among Italians lessened as they emphasized a common Italian culture.[159]

Most historians have documented a steep increase in anti-immigration sentiment in the 1920s, but often depict ethnic communities in almost complete isolation from one another.[160] In Milwaukee, interactions with other ethnic groups were not only noteworthy, but also vital for ethnic communities, especially new immigrants. Like other American cities, Milwaukee attracted large numbers of Italian immigrants in the 1890s, increasingly from southern Italy and Sicily as Italians left behind worsening economic conditions. Despite high clusters of individuals by ethnicity, Milwaukee further demonstrates that it is erroneous to argue that individuals or ethnic communities existed in a vacuum.

Rather than being a homogenous community set apart from the rest of its surroundings, oral history testimony from first- and second-generation Italian residents in Milwaukee reveals that these ethnic communities contained a great deal of diversity and the experiences of these immigrants varied greatly, especially after World War I. These experiences varied with regards to housing, employment patterns and gender roles in these communities. Though there certainly were experiences common to many Italian-Americans in Milwaukee, the range of the experiences in this community makes it impossible to claim that there was a uniform all-encompassing Italian-American experience in Milwaukee.

Milwaukee's early Italian settlements such as the Third Ward consisted overwhelmingly of Sicilians, while the significantly smaller Bay View Italian community attracted northern and central Italians. Due to a variety of forces—such as a shift in housing ideals among Italian immigrants, the reduced availability and deteriorated state of housing in the Third Ward and greater economic mobility—Italians began establishing new "ethnic enclaves" like the First Ward in the 1920s. This process accelerated during the 1930s as the Great Depression left many unemployed and stuck in deteriorating housing conditions.

Italian Housing Patterns in Milwaukee

A study by Donna Gabbacia, which describes housing ideals among Sicilian proverbs and the correlation between satisfaction and resentment by Italians living in Sicily, provides a close comparison of housing conditions in Milwaukee's Italian community due to its very heavy Sicilian presence. These Sicilian proverbs from the 1880s emphasized the importance of homeownership "as little as it is, so long as it's mine"; the importance of living on the second floor or higher to ensure privacy and comfort "one never knows what will come raining down on one's head from above"; and the medical importance of having well-lit rooms because "dark houses bring the doctor."[161]

Despite these aspirations, over half of the properties in Gabaccia's study town, Sambuca di Sicilia, were one-story houses with only two rooms, were poorly lit, had low resale value and had dirt floors. Therefore, many Sicilians were not only disappointed in terms of their economic position, but their housing situation as well.[162] To remedy this situation, many "migrants left Sicily not to establish familiar social ties elsewhere, but to build lives both economically and socially more satisfying than the ones they left behind."[163] The residential patterns utilized by Milwaukee's Italian immigrants reflected their motivations to achieve some of these housing ideals, and their ability to make such decisions often was impacted by Milwaukee's residential and economic opportunities.

As previously stated, most of Milwaukee's Italians lived in the Third Ward. Italian residents within the Third Ward noted that they had inherited the neighborhood from the Irish who had lived there during an earlier period of immigration.[164] Many Italians moved into the area since cheap housing became available after a fire swept through the predominantly Irish neighborhood on October 28, 1892, burning over half the ward as well as razing 465 homes and killing four people.[165]

While a minority of Milwaukee's Italians lived among other ethnic groups, such as the Germans, the majority lived in the Third Ward. The number of Italians in Milwaukee rose from only several hundred in 1890 to 1,740 in 1900 and 4,788 in 1910.[166] By 1910, 90 percent of Milwaukee's Italian immigrants came from southern Italy, 98 percent of whom were Sicilian.[167] Despite similar origins, residents often encountered communication problems when interacting with one another.[168] Linguistic problems arose often since Italians had emigrated from a country in which "there were either 13 or 14 different ethnic groups."[169] The difficulty in creating language as an Italian unifier has proven problematic in Italy as well. A majority of Italians spoke in dialects other than the "official" Tuscan dialect even as of 2007.[170]

Though Milwaukee's Third Ward saw an increasing concentration of Italians after 1900 and was dubbed "Little Italy" by its residents, "the notion that Milwaukee's Third Ward after the fire of 1892 became populated almost exclusively by Italians" is in fact a "historical misconception." Though Milwaukee's Italian community, with its largest concentration in the Third Ward, established its own highly visible institutions, even by 1910 the 2,759 Italians living in the Third Ward comprised less than half of the Third Ward's total population.[171]

Historian Mark Choate has astutely argued that "the social and economic divisions between northern and southern Italians were replicated in their colonies overseas."[172] While the controversy regarding the placement of a northern Italian priest at Our Lady of Pompeii (mentioned in chapter two) has been described as "little more than a bump in the road," regional differences did cause some cleavages in Milwaukee's Italian-American population, particularly within the first generation.[173] For example, the overwhelmingly numerous Sicilian residents in the Third Ward organized streets in Italian neighborhoods based on their native towns or cities in Italy. Immigrants from Porticello settled on Cass Street, those from Santo Stefano di Camastra settled on Milwaukee Street and immigrants from Bari lived on

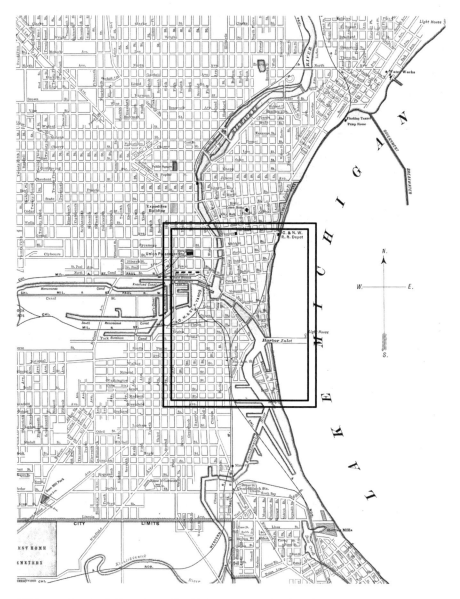

1892 map showing Milwaukee's Third Ward. *From the American Geographical Society Library, University of Wisconsin–Milwaukee Libraries.*

Defining Urban Milwaukee, 1892–1939

Jefferson Street. Other than the Third Ward, there were over one thousand Italians in the Bay View section of Milwaukee whose residents had come mostly from central Italy and Piedmont.[174]

The geographic limits of the Third Ward were Wisconsin Avenue to the north, the Milwaukee River to the west and south and Lake Michigan to the east.[175] Milwaukee's first- and second-generation Italian-American population in the Third Ward found employment in unskilled labor and by establishing small ethnic businesses. Some, such as Gaetanina Balisteri's father, found work near the Third Ward as coal workers and crane operators.[176] Other Italians found employment working on sewage systems, laying railroad tracks and other manual labor activities.[177] These unskilled labor jobs were some of the lowest paying jobs in the city, and workers typically received wages between $1.50 and $2.00 per day.[178] While these various manual labor jobs went almost exclusively to men, women also found employment in the community.

Typically tile and terrazzo workers or steel mill employees, Bay View's Italian residents from central and northern Italy and the Third Ward's mostly Sicilian residents were "as different in many characteristics as the native north of Mason and Dixon's line differs from the native of the southern states."[179] These two Italian communities in Milwaukee were characterized by differences in sources of employment, regional origin and popular culture and, therefore, developed more or less independently of one another during their early years.

Despite these differences, about 75 percent of the Italians employed in the city in 1915 worked as manual laborers.[180] Like their Italian counterparts in the Third Ward, Bay View Italians also had ethnic businesses such as the grocery store, opened in 1912 by Giocando Groppi, which served as the heart of the early Bay View Italian community.[181] Likewise, Garibaldi's tavern was the home to the Giuseppe Garibaldi Mutual Aid Society and sponsored events such as the Garibaldi picnic every summer. Former Bay View resident Mabel Zanchetti also recalled that every Friday a fish salesman named Tarantino would yell *"pesce fresca, pesce fresca,"* or "fresh fish," from the back of his truck in Bay View's Little Italy and sell his wares to Italian women.[182]

Access and affordability to housing contributed to patterns of development among Italian-American immigrants. In terms of housing conditions, the Third Ward was among the worst in the city, and some houses were never repaired after the 1892 fire. The Italian pattern of "chain migration," in which Italians would make return trips to Italy and bring along family members with them upon their return to Milwaukee, contributed to

57

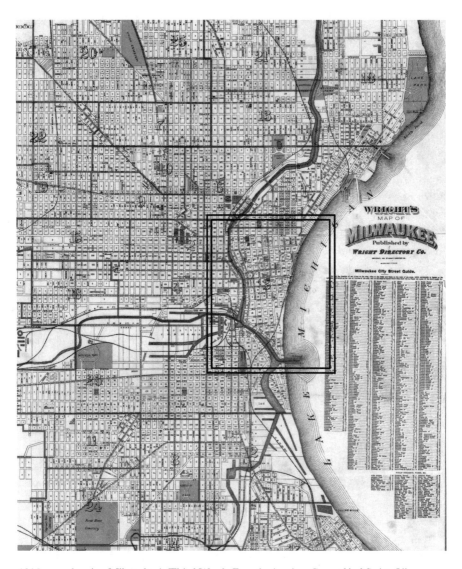

1916 map showing Milwaukee's Third Ward. *From the American Geographical Society Library, University of Wisconsin–Milwaukee Libraries.*

overcrowding, which was accentuated by the 1895 arrival of Sicilians from Chicago.[183] A 1906 study on the Third Ward concluded that some houses in the Third Ward "have been sold and moved to other lots to make way for office buildings or factories which tower many stories above their humble neighbors, and sometimes almost surround them. These houses are, for the most part, in an extreme state of dilapidation." [184] The housing situation in the Third Ward was so bad that it was deemed a public menace to "health and morals" in 1911.[185]

An immigration officer inspecting one Third Ward house in 1910 found the dwelling to contain dark rooms and leaking pipes. He also saw "a friendly goat…playing with the baby on the floor" in a scene very similar to the one painted by a Milwaukee visitor to Naples in 1896, mentioned in chapter two. In this single dwelling lived "one man, two women, ten children, six dogs, two goats, five pigeons, two horses, and other animal life which escaped our hurried observation."[186] The dirtiness of this house was somewhat isolated, as a 1915 report on the 149 poorest Italian families in Milwaukee revealed that 87 houses were in "good cleanliness," 19 were "fair" and 28 were "bad."[187] While the cleanliness of the houses was somewhat isolated, the deteriorating infrastructure was not. Another study on Third Ward housing conducted by the Wisconsin Bureau of Labor in 1912 concluded that the conditions in the Third Ward were the most crowded and poorly structured in Milwaukee.[188]

The attractions of the Third Ward to Italian immigrants were its initially cheap rent, its proximity to places of employment and its location near rail lines. In exchange for living in the shabby housing conditions discussed above, landlords charged an average monthly rent of twelve dollars in the Third Ward. Landlords made very little effort to improve the infrastructure since the Third Ward was increasingly converted into industrial factories and other businesses, further aggravating overcrowding.[189] To demonstrate the difficulties this placed upon an immigrant, a laborer working seven days a week for the Milwaukee Electric Railway and Light Company made thirteen dollars weekly and paid ten dollars per month for a place on Jefferson Street in the 1920s.[190]

In this sense, the industrial transformation occurring in the Third Ward was similar to the experiences of New York City's Italians. Like their Milwaukee counterparts, Italian immigrants in New York City paid about $12.50 per month in rent and also saw buildings near the Italian neighborhood converted into warehouses in the 1880s and 1890s.[191] By 1924 the residential options available to Italian immigrants in Milwaukee shrunk to only ten blocks, upon which six thousand Italians lived in tight quarters![192]

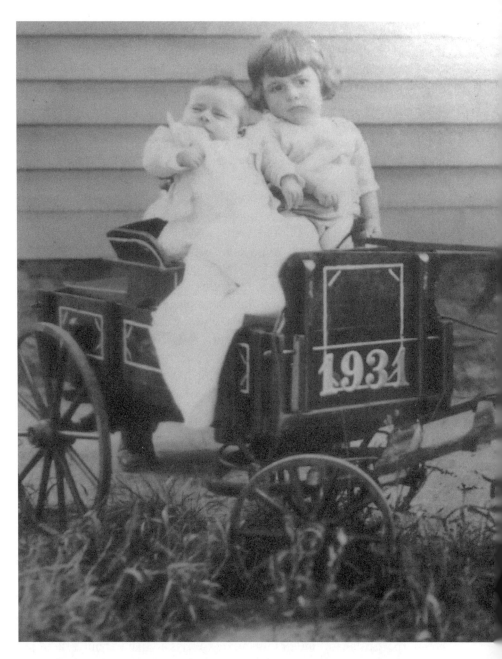

During the Great Depression, it was still common for Italian children in Milwaukee to share their play areas with goats and other farm animals. *Photo courtesy of the Italian Community Center of Milwaukee.*

Defining Urban Milwaukee, 1892–1939

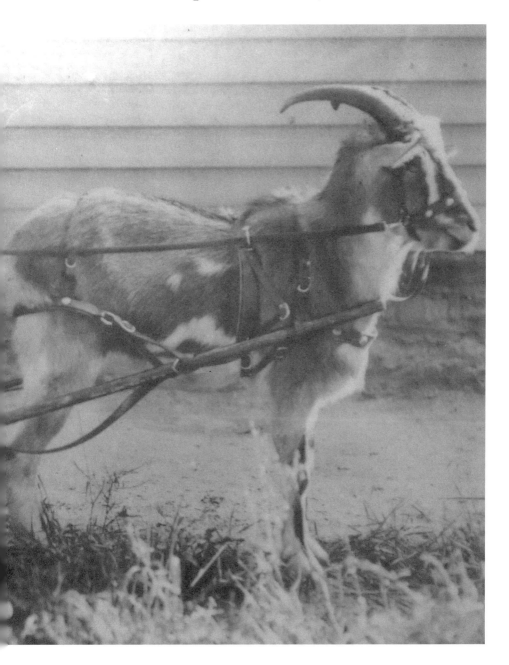

The housing patterns and decisions made by Milwaukee's Italians were impacted by their experiences and housing ideals in Italy as well as their economic situations, contributing to changes after the 1920s. The pattern of densely populated buildings occurred due to economic necessities as Milwaukee's Italians typically found work in unskilled labor jobs as sanitation workers, streetcar company employees or on the railroad. Of 114 Italians working for the city between 1896 and 1913, 103 served in unskilled positions.[193] Though the housing conditions may seem unfathomable to many today, to an Italian immigrant in the early 1900s "being able to live here in Milwaukee in four or five-room apartments with indoor plumbing, regardless of their condition, was a huge improvement over what they left behind in Italy."[194]

Poor plumbing, or even an absence of plumbing, was eased by the proximity of the Third Ward to Lake Michigan. The water situation was a vast improvement from the Sicilian countryside, in which water resources were not easily accessible and water collection proved to be time consuming.[195] Furthermore, the Sicilian housing ideals coincided much more closely with Milwaukee's housing situation than Italy's. Milwaukee's vertically designed housing allowed Italian immigrants to achieve a greater degree of privacy than Sicilian homes and made it much easier to travel to work every day, unlike the long distances that Italian peasants were required to travel in Sicily.

The housing practices of the mostly Sicilian Third Ward in Milwaukee fit in very well with Donna Gabaccia's argument that the first generation of Italian immigrants' primary housing focus was to achieve social satisfaction balanced with some of the housing ideals. The second generation of Milwaukee's Italians, just as New York City's Italians, was more concerned with attaining better housing conditions than with the housing ideals that were common among first-generation immigrants. While still valuing ethnic ties, Milwaukee's Italians began to privilege improved housing amenities over kinship connections.[196] By the 1920s, Italians began moving to the First Ward and elsewhere in Milwaukee to seek better housing when economically possible, which resulted in the continuing dispersal of the Italians in Milwaukee. However, the Great Depression complicated this process, and those remaining in the Third Ward encountered very difficult circumstances.

Defining Urban Milwaukee, 1892–1939

The First Ward: Brady Street

The deteriorating housing situation in the Third Ward, along with more economic opportunities elsewhere, led to a slow but increasing trend of settlement in the First Ward. Though only forty-five Italian-born immigrants lived in the First Ward in 1910, it received an influx of both new immigrants and former Third Ward residents in the decades to follow.[197] Also, southern Italians and Sicilians, who sought better housing conditions in the city, began to move to the First Ward from the Third Ward in larger waves starting in 1918.[198]

The desire to obtain better conditions along with scarce housing availability in the Third Ward persuaded those who had the means to do so to move around the Brady Street neighborhood in Milwaukee's First Ward. The steep decline in return migration among Italian migrants after World War I, combined with favoring better housing conditions over settling extensively with residents from a similar region, led to significant housing changes among Italian-Americans. The impact of return migration's decline can be seen in the extremely high rate of homeownership in the United States by 1930 among Italian-Americans compared to other ethnic groups.[199] Given the correlation between the decline of return migration and the subsequent increase in homeownership, the move to the First Ward can be seen not only as an economic and cultural response to changing conditions, but also as a symbolic declaration among Italian immigrants to state their intention of creating a life in the United States for themselves and their families.

After emigrating from Sicily in 1893, Tom Busalacchi's father worked in Milwaukee as a fruit peddler, a foreman for a streetcar company and then owned a tavern until he opened the Milwaukee Macaroni Company in Milwaukee with two friends in 1911. The macaroni factory became very successful and had markets throughout Wisconsin and parts of Illinois and Michigan.[200] After several moves and a name change to Busalacchi Brothers Macaroni Manufacturing Company, the factory was located on 155 Huron Street in 1923.[201] Despite the factory's location in the Third Ward, the Busalacchi family moved to Oakland Avenue on the East Side in 1916.[202] This anecdote is both an anomaly and a good illustration of some changes in Milwaukee's Italian community in the 1920s and beyond.

Despite Busalacchi's family living on the East Side, the factory remained in the Third Ward until 1939 and employed about twenty-five to thirty Italian residents in the Third Ward.[203] The entrepreneurial success enjoyed from the macaroni factory was very much an exception as Milwaukee's Italians remained overwhelmingly working class. Oswaldo Natrelli's father offers a more typical move to the First Ward. After arriving in the United States from the Abruzzo province in central Italy in the 1920s, he settled on Marshall Street, near a large concentration of Italian-Americans on Brady Street, and worked as a miner for a water sewage company.[204]

Despite a shift by some Italian residents from the Third Ward and Bay View to the East Side, many Italians remained in the Third Ward. Furthermore, important connections remained between the Italian community in the Third Ward and the growing presence of Italians in the First Ward. As Italians increasingly left the Third Ward for the First Ward in the 1920s, friends and relatives often remained in contact through social organizations and popular culture that will be explored in more detail in chapter five. Often, Italians residing on the East Side or Bay View returned to the Third Ward to attend religious services at Our Lady of Pompeii Parish.[205] Pompeii's 1934 parish records indicate that in addition to Italian families in the Third Ward such as the Emanuele, Glorioso, Machi and Pizzino families, the Gardetto and Groppi families of Bay View, along with the Natarelli and Sorgi families of the First Ward, attended.[206] The overwhelmingly Italian congregation at Pompeii from various Italian neighborhoods corresponded to the rise of a greater Italian identity in Milwaukee during the 1920s and 1930s.[207]

As Italians increasingly settled in the First Ward, they maintained cultural connections through family, friends, ethnic stores and religion, yet also shared the neighborhood with other recent immigrant groups such as Poles and Jews.[208] By the 1930s, it was clear that the main concentration of the Italian community had shifted to the First Ward, as evidenced by the fact that 705 of 1,200 families belonging to Pompeii lived on the East Side, resulting in the building of the larger St. Rita's Church there by 1939.[209]

The shift to the First Ward was evident even earlier, as the 1,398 Italians living in the First Ward outnumbered the 1,154 Italians living in the Third Ward in 1930.[210] By 1930 more Italians were living on Milwaukee's East Side than in the Third Ward because they sought better housing conditions and economic opportunities. However, the Great Depression hit in 1929 and would continue to have a significant impact on the daily lives of the Italian community as it imposed dramatic economic hardships. As recent arrivals to the United States, Milwaukee's Italians, like other minority groups of that era, were hit especially hard.

Defining Urban Milwaukee, 1892–1939

Housing Conditions and Unemployment during the Great Depression

As mostly unskilled workers, Milwaukee's Italian residents were among the first to be laid off when production slowed down in the 1930s. After many residents in the Third Ward were laid off from industrial jobs, some eventually found work through the New Deal's Works Project Administration (WPA).[211] Likewise, Italians in the First Ward also found work through the WPA and served as tunnel workers during the Great Depression.[212] The widespread poverty during the Great Depression produced dramatic scenes. According to former Third Ward resident Peter Pizzino, when his father, Basilio, waited outside the Brumer Building for one of only four jobs, he was joined by thousands of fellow applicants, including many German, Chinese, Mexican, Italian and Polish immigrants.[213]

In between periods of employment, Italian women expanded their economic influence, as will be demonstrated in chapter four. However, there were times when Italians had to apply for and accept charities such as food stamps and other necessities. Milwaukee's Italians often resisted doing this since it "was considered a disgrace to seek help from outside one's family circle" in Italy.[214] Instead, the Italian community attempted to take up collections to assist unemployed families as an alternative to the perceived shame they associated with accepting public foodstuffs of flour, cereal, beans and other goods.[215] However, with widespread poverty throughout the community and Milwaukee, there were few alternatives. Many Italians accepted the food staples and placed them on wagons to be hauled from downtown Milwaukee's municipal buildings to a resident's house, in a very embarrassing process.[216]

Families such as Vincent Emanuele's encountered declining infrastructure combined with economic difficulties. Living on 235 North Jefferson Street in a flat with his parents and seven younger siblings, Vincent found his family sharing "three bedrooms, a dining room" and a kitchen.[217] Many of the buildings in the neighborhood experienced freezing pipes in winter, were dilapidated and literally "leaned against each other."[218] Such extreme conditions earned the tenement section of the Third Ward the nickname "palazzo porcile," or "pigsty palace."[219] The "palazzo" apartments often were severely overcrowded and commonly contained rats, bed bugs and cockroaches. The aging Third Ward houses also did not have bathtubs, only a "wash tub on the porch, or a sink in the house with only a cold water faucet." It was not uncommon for up to five families to share outhouses, as most homes lacked hot water and often experienced freezing pipes in the winter.[220] Housing conditions such as those encountered by the Emanuele family differed greatly from those Italians living outside of the Third Ward.

As with the various other experiences documented earlier, Milwaukee's Italians experienced a heterogeneous housing experience during the Great Depression. In contrast to the Emanuele family, the Gagliano family lived in a duplex on Twenty-seventh and Clybourn and did not face the housing conditions that those in older tenement houses encountered.[221] Grace Falbo, Nick Gagliano's daughter, lived in an ethnically mixed neighborhood containing mostly German and Irish residents. Like the Gagliano family, the Bertolas family also lived in an ethnically diverse neighborhood on Jackson and obtained a three-bedroom place in better shape than those found in "palazzo porcile."[222] Access to decent housing was connected to access to dependable and consistent employment.

Unlike the working-class Bertolas family or the middle-class Gagliano family, the Emanuele family's economic situation was far from settled. At the time of living in poor housing conditions, Vincent's father was unemployed for three years once the Depression began. Compounding this problem was the fact that the family members were recent arrivals to Milwaukee from Cleveland. Once his father found employment through the Works Progress Administration under the New Deal, the family moved to Cass Street in the First Ward to a house with heat and a private bathroom.[223] Though sometimes nostalgically remembered as a bastion for Italian-Americans, the Third Ward featured significant housing problems. Residents of the Third Ward did not choose to live there solely based on ethnic ties; they were also constricted by their economic conditions, which often dictated remaining in substandard housing in older sections of the city.

An Urban Community:
Expanding Ethnic Interaction

Milwaukee, like other cities with large immigrant populations, certainly was not isolated.[224] The housing situation and the relocation of a significant portion of Milwaukee's Italian population between 1900 and 1940 displayed the changing perceptions and attitudes toward housing in accordance with greater economic opportunities as time progressed. In Sicily, most rural towns were geographically isolated because they were located between five and twenty-five kilometers away from one another, and socially isolated since residents of neighboring towns viewed one another as enemies.[225] Unlike the isolated rural towns in Italy, from which some of Milwaukee's Italian immigrants originated, it was not possible to "meet the challenges posed by the dynamic urban society into which the new arrivals were plunged" without making modifications to their environment.[226]

In other words, immigrants were "compelled to have extensive contact with 'outsiders' in their community" as a mechanism of "survival in an urban environment."[227] It would be historically inaccurate to conclude that "within a decade of settlement in Milwaukee's Third Ward, Italians had created the most homogenous ethnic community in the city," as historians have in the past, without further clarification.[228]

Such proclamations are not without certain elements of truth. Milwaukee's Italians did live in densely congregated neighborhoods in which friends and relatives from Italy would live together based on their region of origin. Also, as previously mentioned, Italian immigrants established banks, their own church, ethnic businesses and cultural practices. However, Milwaukee's Italians also interacted with other ethnic groups through residential patterns, economic interactions and cultural events.

As previously stated, Milwaukee's Italians often lived in densely populated housing complexes in which they sometimes took in boarders. This practice has been characterized by historians as the "peculiar Italian-American invention of giving refuge to numerous boarders," which "aggravated the existing problem of overcrowding." [229] In 1910 about 40 percent of Italian homes took in boarders, both Italian and non-Italian. In addition to providing a room, Italian women also provided food and laundry to guests in exchange for money. As time progressed, it became increasingly rare for Italians to practice boarding, possibly explained by the end of large-scale emigration from Italy in 1924, as well as the decline in the number of single males arriving after 1911.[230] While the practice declined, it was still maintained occasionally during the Great Depression.

The dramatic decline of the American economy in the 1930s led to unprecedented unemployment, as even doctors found themselves without work. One such doctor temporarily boarded in the Pizzino household, where he stayed in exchange for treating ill residents in the neighborhood. Likewise, an unemployed African American couple, James Musten and his wife, lived in the same household for five dollars per week and provided cooking assistance. After a boarder obtained a job, he typically moved out immediately, and James Musten was no exception; he found a construction

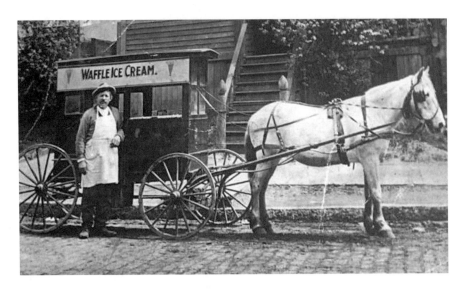

Peddling offered Italian immigrants a livelihood and encouraged interaction with non-Italians. *Photo courtesy of the Italian Community Center of Milwaukee.*

job and moved to Walnut Street shortly thereafter.[231] Even so, the Italian practice of taking in boarders shifted from taking in generally single Italian males in the first decade of the twentieth century to an economic activity involving Milwaukee's other ethnic groups.

While the great majority of Italian immigrants were unskilled laborers, small local businesses were common in Milwaukee's Italian-American community and increased the interaction between the Italian communities and the larger Milwaukee community. Local taverns operated by fellow Italians within the Third Ward, along with small shoe stores such as Maniaci's, were common.[232] Small grocery stores—such as those operated by the Balisteris—often specialized in particular foods and other assorted goods. LeRoy Bertocini's grandfather established Corti's, which sold goods to passengers in between train rides near the Northwestern train depot. Customers would purchase homemade ice cream and candy at Corti's along with cigars and other tobacco products.[233]

In addition to formal business establishments, informal trading took place at the railroad tracks as it was common for Italians to obtain five or six "burlap sacks with coal," which could be used to heat homes, from the engineer in exchange for homemade Italian red wine.[234] In Bay View, ethnic Italian stores served the dual purpose of preserving traditional Italian cuisine while also introducing it to new customers. For example, one Italian

Defining Urban Milwaukee, 1892–1939

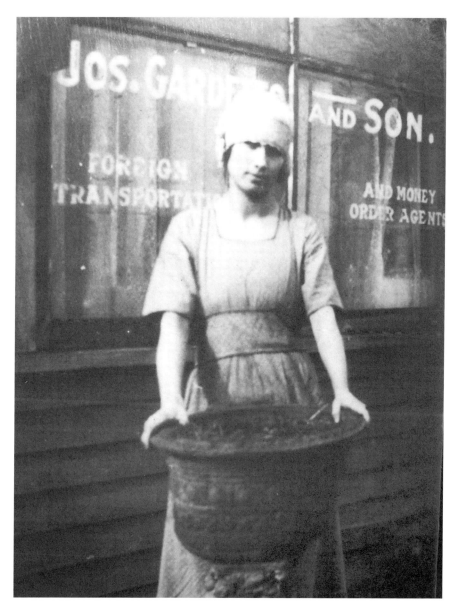

A young woman outside the Gardetto establishment in Bay View, 1920. The Gardettos ran a combination saloon, bakery and travel agency on St. Clair Avenue. *Photo courtesy of the Italian Community Center of Milwaukee.*

family in Bay View did all of their grocery shopping at Groppi's in the mid-1930s, and like many of their predominantly German and Polish neighbors in Bay View, they received fresh bread from Gardetto's bakery several times a week.[235] Interactions with non-Italian Milwaukeeans were not limited to these brief purchases.

The organization of small Italian-run businesses necessitated interaction with other ethnic groups. Nick Gagliano and his business partner served as fruit peddlers specializing in bananas. To expand their business, Nick obtained distributors who had access to larger markets. Milwaukee's Jews were often the suppliers and merchants who worked with Nick Gagliano and operated well-known stores within Milwaukee such as Kohl's, Crystal Market and Lerner's.[236] Business relationships such as those between Italians such as Gagliano and Jewish distributors were mutually beneficial and necessary for small suppliers to improve economically.

Meaningful relationships between Italian-Americans and other ethnic groups were not exclusive to suppliers. Tony Seidita's father, Joe, established Joe Seidita and Company in the early 1920s along with his brother-in-law Jack Sibrigandio. According to Tony, the store was "the first combination store in the heart of the Third Ward," selling not just

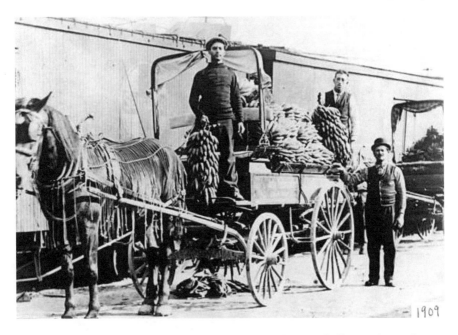

The wholesale produce business encouraged cooperation between Italian vendors and Jewish grocers in Milwaukee in the early twentieth century. *Photo courtesy of the Italian Community Center of Milwaukee.*

Defining Urban Milwaukee, 1892–1939

fruits and vegetables but groceries and meat as well.[237] In conjunction with the New Immigrants from Europe, Mexican-Americans primarily took manual labor jobs in Milwaukee and found employment working on railroads.[238] Tony Seidita, then a young boy, recalled that "we used to deliver to them at night and the very first I can remember, we used to deliver along a railroad on the south side, just over the Broadway Street Bridge." Tony described the Mexicans as "all good customers, all good people, hard workers," but observed that the community was almost exclusively male in the 1920s.[239]

Similarly, fruit peddler Joe Renello often went to Wauwatosa near Sixtieth Street and Bluemound Road to sell fruits, meats and other Italian cuisine from Italian grocers in the Third Ward to French, Italians, Germans, Croatians and Greeks. On the same trip, Renello bought eggs from farms in Wauwatosa and then sold them back in the Third Ward.[240]

In addition to economic and residential interactions with other ethnic groups in Milwaukee, there also were dynamic cultural and intellectual exchanges. Italian consul Angelo Cerminara spoke to the Jewish congregation at Temple Emanu-E B'ne Jeshurun on Prospect and Kenwood on the topic of "The Youth Movement in Italy."[241] Similarly, at a celebration of the Beulah Brinton Community House's opening, featuring mostly Italian speakers and entertainment, a Mexican String Quartet performed alongside Bay View Italians at a concert on October 14, 1924.

This event is noteworthy on several fronts. The event was attended by Milwaukee Mayor Daniel Hoan and local school and political representatives, with no ethnic groups other than Italians or Mexicans present.[242] This is even more remarkable since according to church records, fewer than three hundred Mexicans lived in Milwaukee by May 1926.[243] Provi Jendusa, whose parents immigrated to Milwaukee from Balestrate, Sicily, in 1908, recalled that life for immigrants and their children often "wasn't easy…and other ethnic groups went through the exact same process that we did."[244] Just as the Irish gradually were replaced in the Third Ward by the Italians and Greeks beginning in the 1890s, newer immigrant groups such as Mexicans very slowly began establishing a greater cultural presence in Milwaukee, especially the near South Side.

Founded by Beulah Brinton, the wife of a steel mill employee, the center on Saint Clair Street and East Potter Avenue in Bay View offered English language classes for adults, sewing classes for women and girls and sports activities for children. Furthermore, Ann Magnarini recalled that movies were shown and dinner events were held there.[245]

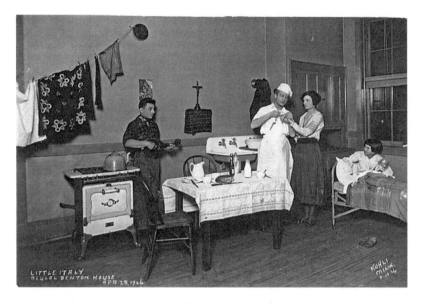

Cultural activities at the Beulah Brinton House in Bay View—such as this 1926 play—encouraged Americanization among immigrants. *Photo courtesy of Tim Kenney, Giuseppe Garibaldi Society of Milwaukee.*

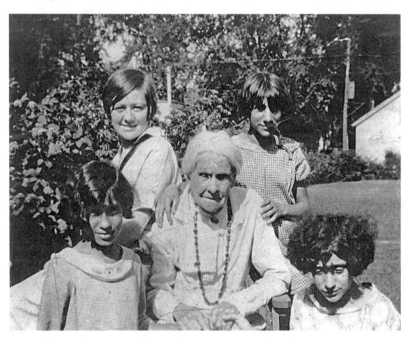

Top row: Miss Gordon and Hilda Basile. *Bottom row*: unknown, Beulah Brinton and Ang. Basile. *Photo courtesy of Tim Kenney, Giuseppe Garibaldi Society of Milwaukee.*

Defining Urban Milwaukee, 1892–1939

In 1912 Milwaukee established social centers, which provided education classes and an opportunity for immigrants to learn languages, as well as cultural events, naturalization preparation and other activities. Amazingly, the leaders of these institutions "even organized 'tours of understanding' in which one ethnic group of older children visited the ethnic neighborhood of another group." With the goal of showcasing businesses and cultural attractions in the Italian community, "after the tours, the group of either Polish, German, or Irish children were served an Italian meal at the center" and watched Italian "marches and folk dances."[246]

The support of Milwaukee's city government was instrumental in orchestrating such exchanges. Leading Milwaukee Socialists such as Mayor Emil Seidel and city attorney Daniel Hoan not only paid lip service to their support of immigrants, but also successfully convinced the Wisconsin legislature in 1911 to tax Milwaukeeans to finance such social centers. Furthermore, by the 1920s, Milwaukee was the first American city to integrate and affiliate these social centers within the city's public school system.[247]

This tradition continued through the decades in Milwaukee's Third Ward, as Milwaukeeans visited the Italian neighborhood in 1935 on behalf of the

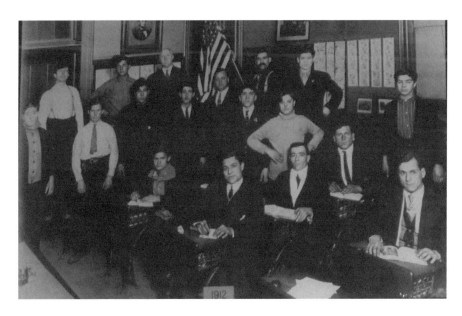

With the decline of return migration, more Italians chose to become American citizens. Naturalization classes helped prepare them for a permanent future in the United States. *Photo courtesy of the Italian Community Center of Milwaukee.*

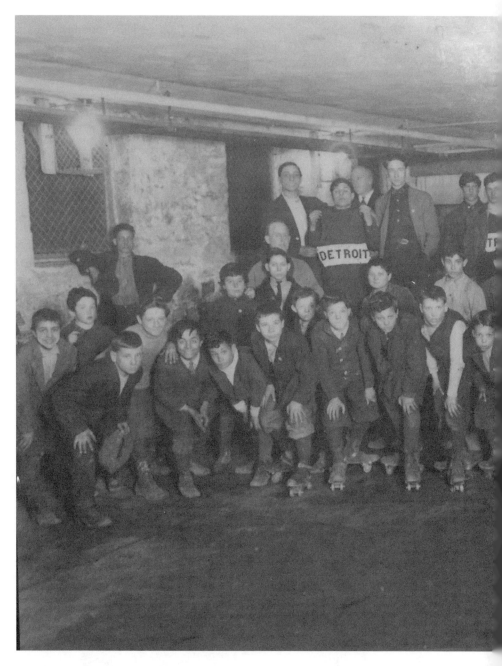

Second-generation Italian-Americans in Milwaukee were encouraged to play and interact with non-Italians at local community centers, accelerating Americanization. *Photo courtesy of the Italian Community Center of Milwaukee.*

Defining Urban Milwaukee, 1892–1939

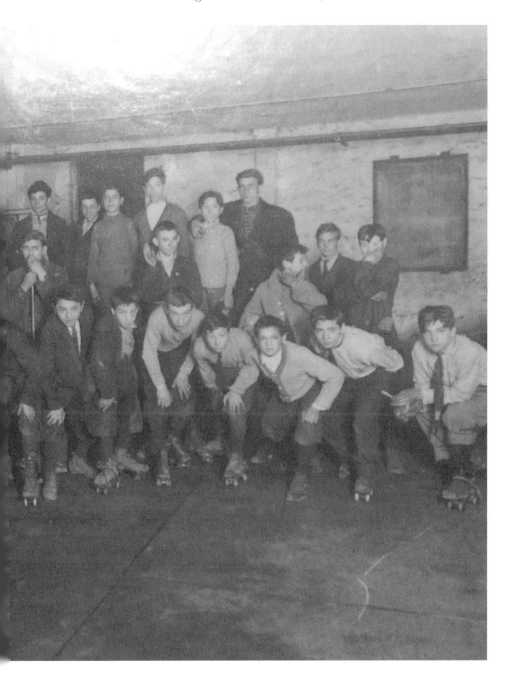

Italian community and the Milwaukee Race Relations Council—just as they had the African American, Greek and Jewish neighborhoods in 1934. In addition to "touring" the Italian neighborhoods and sampling Italian pastries and cuisine, other ethnic groups were treated to Italian music and hand-woven art by Italian women at the Andrew Jackson Social Center in the Third Ward.[248] Rather than being an isolated community, the Italian community in Milwaukee became increasingly interactive with other ethnic groups by the 1920s. All of these revelations display not only more extensive interactions between ethnic communities, but also a blurring of geographical boundaries within the city.

Discrimination

Based upon the testimonies of Milwaukee's Italian-American residents, there does not appear to have been any widespread anti-Italian sentiment in the city. However, several interviewees reported anti-immigrant sentiment tied to geography, as well as their connection to other members of the New Immigration. According to Vincent Emanuele, non-Italians in Milwaukee would make reference to the Third Ward containing "Dagos." Furthermore, when working his paper route, his friend's father told his son to put on a new shirt to avoid looking like "one of those guys from the ward."[249]

In addition to ethnic slurs, religious slurs were also used. Upon completion of a teaching degree from Marquette University, an Italian man was also told to avoid "certain areas" since someone pointed out "not only that we were Italian or Sicilian, but we were Catholic." However, another person told him that "the way business is, we don't have anything for you, but you're lucky you're Italian and you're not Jewish."[250] After submitting the name of a Jewish friend for the History Honorary Society at Marquette University, Grace Falbo was told that her friend's name would be denied because she was Jewish.[251] The reasoning for non-Italian Milwaukeeans to express openly anti-Semitic perspectives with Italian immigrants is not clear, though it may have been meant as an indirect way to express racist and xenophobic attitudes not only against Jewish-Americans, but also against members of the New Immigration in general.

Defining Urban Milwaukee, 1892–1939

Conclusion

The long-standing regional tensions between northern and southern Italians were replicated in Milwaukee and contributed to the emergence of a distinctly Sicilian Third Ward and a northern and central Italian community in Bay View. The housing conditions encountered by Milwaukee's Italians were among the worst in the city, and living patterns were influenced by economic conditions and housing preferences among initial immigrants. Housing practices, such as accepting boarders, were a departure from practices in Sicily and were a way of extending their contacts in the city, while also earning extra money.[252]

In addition to accepting boarders, increasing numbers of Milwaukee's Italians sought better housing conditions than those found in the Third Ward, and by 1930, the First Ward had more Italian residents than either the Third Ward or Bay View communities. The transition to the First Ward was made astronomically more difficult as the Great Depression created unprecedented unemployment throughout the city. For Italians and other recent arrivals to Milwaukee, the economic situation often determined where immigrants could and did live. A Third Ward resident who lived through the Depression in the Third Ward cautioned not to "let anybody tell you that they were the good old days, because they weren't…we had a ghetto." However, the poverty that many in the Italian community felt also provided the motivational "impetus to do better."[253]

Though still physically located in ethnic enclaves throughout the city, the Italian population of Milwaukee had significant interactions with other Milwaukeeans throughout the community's history in a process that greatly expanded during the 1930s. Their experiences varied in Milwaukee with regards to housing, employment patterns and family roles in these communities. In any case, it is erroneous to conclude as Judith Simonsen has that "Milwaukee's Third Ward became the local center for Italian immigration at the turn of the century, forming a homogenous colony."[254]

The residential, economic and cultural events that were shared by both Bay View Italians and Third Ward residents with other ethnic groups typically involved other New Immigrants. Interactions with Milwaukee's Jewish, Mexican, Polish, African American, German and Irish residents were typically, though not always, established to provide some type of mutual coping mechanism in dealing with an urban environment. My research has not uncovered any widespread overt movement against Italians in the city. At least a partial reason for the absence of an anti-Italian movement in the city can be attributed to the city of Milwaukee's political leaders encouraging a pluralistic city through ethnic interactions. However, some of Milwaukee's non-Italian residents expressed anger over New Immigration as a general phenomenon.

CHAPTER 4

Family Life in Milwaukee's Italian Community

While married with children, Anna Torretta took over Burgerino's, a small grocery store in the Third Ward, from her parents.[255] Despite being illiterate and having a limited grasp of English, Anna produced and sold her own wine, ran a butcher shop connected to the grocery store, performed butchering duties and established a second grocery store—Rampolla, in Shorewood—with her son-in-law![256]

In addition to the immigrant remittances, foreign relations, housing practices and settlement patterns discussed in chapters two and three, the experiences of Italian immigrant women were sharply impacted by their experiences across the Atlantic prior to emigration. Italian women were actively involved in the making of ethnic communities socially, culturally and economically. In her 2006 work, *Merchants, Midwives, and Laboring Women: Italian Migrants in Urban America*, historian Diane Vecchio claims that "Italian women have generally been presented, not as agents, but as passive victims of an intensely patriarchal culture."[257] As Vecchio astutely points out, the economic endeavors of Italian women in Milwaukee refutes such simplistic claims.[258]

In contrast to traditional beliefs about Italian immigrants, Italian women often worked outside the home in paid and unpaid roles. In Milwaukee, Italian women took active roles in ethnic businesses, in social activities throughout the community and in religious activities that enhanced an Italian cultural presence in the city in little-known but fascinating processes. Italian women created unique entrepreneurial opportunities in Milwaukee that differed from other American cities.

Attitudes carried over from Italy regarding education and paid employment for females also contributed to increased burdens and social responsibilities for Italian girls within economically depressed immigrant families. As the second generation of Italians in Milwaukee came of age, the Italian cultural ties were enhanced, while some of the traditional social practices such as dating and courtship weakened in the 1930s and 1940s.

Women in Italy

Knowledge of the economic circumstances of Italian women prior to emigration is essential to obtain a better evaluation of economic endeavors upon arrival in the United States. Records on Sicilian women in the 1880s indicate that many were employed as spinners, weavers, servants, tailors and midwives and combined these occupations with domestic activities. This was influenced by Sicilian ideals, which dictated that the father was in charge of guiding a family's economic endeavors along with ensuring that his wife and daughters maintain a monogamous lifestyle. Similarly, the mother was praised as a housekeeper and as the maintainer of the house, and she was also in charge of arranging her children's marriages.[259] Despite these ideals, the environment in Italy made it very rare to realize many of these idealized family roles.

Maintaining the family was by no means a routine one and often contradicted gender ideals. While upper-class women in Sicilian towns were able to remain inside, much of the population in villages was steeped in extreme poverty. Therefore, daily activities such as cooking, obtaining firewood and other endeavors made it "absolutely impossible for a poorer woman to accomplish many of her household chores while remaining in her home," as she often had to purchase these items throughout the day.[260] During much of the year, Italian men employed as agricultural laborers had to travel long distances to reach the fields in which they worked. This made it difficult for Italian men to establish meaningful social ties, maintain knowledge of their family's activities and control the family economy.[261] Likewise, American visitors were shocked to see many poorer northern Italian women "plowing, haying, carrying heavy loads of hay…grinding their own grains on hand mills, making their own bread, raising small animals…and processing food."[262]

It was not uncommon for Italian men to be physically present in the village only once per week while working as laborers.[263] As a result, very "few peasant fathers then actually directed their families collective economic endeavors."[264] Daily circumstances in the peasant villages where many Italians lived dictated that women be given a great deal of independence.

While Italian women were considerably more powerful in running the day-to-day activities of their families, they faced educational and economic disadvantages. As chapter one pointed out, illiteracy was a major problem for Italy in the nineteenth century, especially in southern Italy. Illiteracy remained particularly entrenched as a major problem for Italian women as only one-third of Italian women could read or write.[265] Maintaining literacy was also problematic; many Italian women who did learn to read and write often fell back into illiteracy because many southern Italian households did not contain reading materials within the home. Men were not as affected by this phenomenon since mandatory military service required Italian men to be literate eventually.[266] Additionally, within some Italian families there was a belief that educating girls was a waste of the family's scarce resources, as Italy lacked free public schools.[267] Finally, impoverished Italian families were sometimes hesitant to encourage female education since skills like sewing offered an impoverished family a greater chance of extra income than literacy did, in the short term.[268] Despite other advantages, education remained a significant hurdle for many Italian women.

The practices of Italian women participating in paid or unpaid home work along with educational scarcity contributed to employment patterns in Italy. In the 1870s only about 10 percent of immigrant women to the United States, Italian or otherwise, had occupations. By 1900 about 30 percent of immigrant women in the United States had occupations in their country of origin, most often as domestic servants.[269] The gender imbalance in employment proved difficult for immigrant women, since in 1882 the United States denied entrance to individuals who may eventually be unable to support themselves. The implication of this law was that immigrant women could be denied or turned away since they were believed by many Americans to be dependents. At the same time, American immigration policy also dictated family unification as a key component.[270]

However, immigrant women arrived with skills that have yet to be explored fully by historians. For example, women made up 48.8 percent of Italians engaged in small-scale retail in Piedmont and 46 percent in both Calabria and Sicily.[271] Nonetheless, American assumptions about gender roles contributed to the notion that immigrant women were inherently dependent upon their husbands or fathers regardless of the realities of the dynamics of gender relations overseas. The experiences of Italian immigrant women would be influenced by Italian ideals, the experiences of family dynamics in Italy and American assumptions about womanhood and the family—all contributing to unique experiences for Milwaukee's Italian-American community.

The Role of Italians in Milwaukee's Economy

In Endicott, New York, many Italian women found significant employment opportunities by working at the Endicott Johnson shoe factory. Italian women took advantage of the separation of genders in the shoe-making process, the proximity of the factory to their homes and the promotion of traditionally "feminine" work similar to other immigrant jobs such as textile work.[272] In contrast, Milwaukee, like Detroit and Buffalo, had a diversified economy "based primarily on heavy industry, which required a male workforce."[273]

Milwaukee also possessed an extremely diverse ethnic composition that restricted some economic opportunities—but also allowed for greater diversity than Endicott's single-industry domination. At the turn of the century, earlier arrivals to Milwaukee such as the British, Germans, Irish and Poles vastly outnumbered the Italians and engaged in ethnic patronage whereby they would give factory jobs by word of mouth to members of their own ethnicity. Similarly, German and Russian Jews established niches for themselves in the garment industries. Though not nearly excluded from higher-paying jobs to the extent that African Americans later were, Italians pursued a combination of low-paying industrial jobs along with establishing ethnic businesses.[274]

As discussed in chapter two, return migration had an astronomical impact on the formation of the Italian community. Of the millions of returning Italian migrants traveling between the Americas and Italy between 1902 and 1910, 90 percent were males, over 90 percent worked as unskilled laborers, 80 percent of returning migrants to Italy had been in the United States for less than five years and most were between the ages of fourteen and forty-four.[275]

Part of the reason for the near monopoly that males had on return migration was that "the most important Italian occupational niche worldwide was that of male construction worker."[276] Italian men worked as "veritable human steam shovels who built the transportation and urban infrastructures of modern capitalism" and built railroads in the Balkans, Argentina and South Africa; worked on the Panama and Suez Canals;

Family Life in Milwaukee's Italian Community

and built railroads, sewers and subways in American cities such as New York City, Philadelphia, Boston, Cleveland and Chicago.[277] In Milwaukee, such a working-class identity was common among Italian males, and the Jendusa family's slogan, "work with a pick, rest with a shovel," summed up the experiences of the majority of Italian males in the community.[278] The only exceptions to these seasonal construction workers were the Italians with permanent work in California's wine vineyards and agricultural work, San Francisco's Italians active in the fishing business and Tampa's Italians active in the fishing and cigar-making businesses.[279]

SHAPING A NEW WORLD: FIRST-GENERATION ENTREPRENEURS

In 1915 only 5 of 149 Italian families in Milwaukee surveyed by George La Piana had women who worked for wages. At the time, it was thought that Milwaukee's Sicilians disliked having Italian females work for strangers and cited the fact that Italian girls often married at age sixteen or seventeen as an obstacle to entering the workforce.[280] Italian women who were employed mostly found work as seamstresses, though a few served as nurses.[281] Even by 1945, it was noted that despite some embroidery work, "the Italian woman, especially the early immigrant, was loath to seek employment outside of her home" and that "the married woman had one all-important occupation, that of being a good mother and wife."[282] However, such simplistic characterizations hid the true role of Italian females in Milwaukee's Italian community.

Despite low employment rates by Italian women in the city, first-generation women in Milwaukee still maintained vital economic activities, whether they were directly compensated or not, and opportunities were structured around employment opportunities in Milwaukee. As Milwaukee began to industrialize more fully after 1900, its economy created a large demand for male labor to perform unskilled tasks in manufacturing and construction. In industries more open to women, such as shoemaking, factories were not located near the Third

Following pages: A construction crew including many Italians at the original Harley-Davidson plant on Thirty-seventh and Juneau in 1915. *Photo courtesy of the Italian Community Center of Milwaukee.*

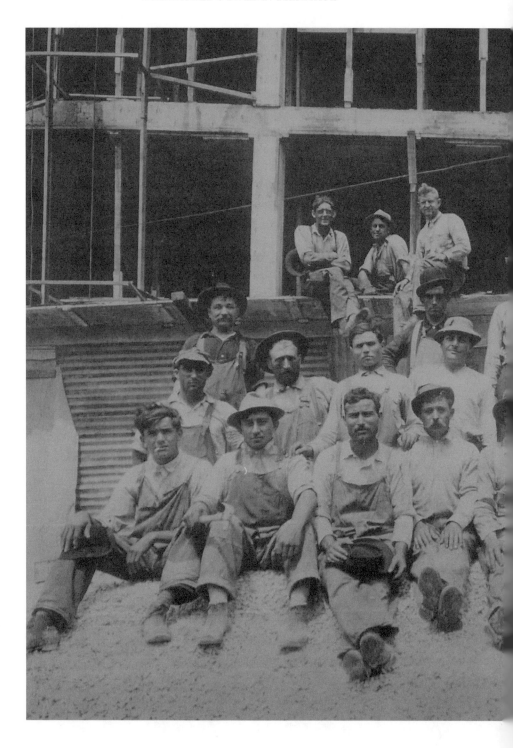

Family Life in Milwaukee's Italian Community

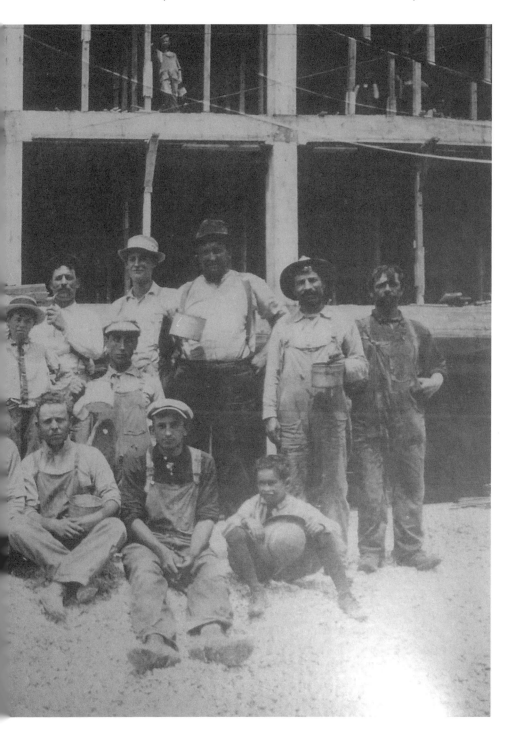

Ward and employed German women as laborers instead.[283] Despite having few women employed outside the home among first-generation immigrants, Italian women along with Jewish women were the most common ethnic groups in which women earned wages through business activities. By meeting the "growing demands and needs of the ethnic enclave" in Milwaukee, Italian women moved beyond conventional definitions of employment and often revealed "their active roles as independent entrepreneurs."[284] Often, these activities centered upon ethnic businesses such as grocery stores, peddling businesses, taverns and other ethnic establishments that also served to strengthen an Italian identity in the city.

The extent of first-generation Italian women's involvement in these enterprises ranged from cooking to serving as business partners with their husbands or fathers to becoming entrepreneurs themselves. For example, after Frank San Filippo established his tavern, The Alamo, on Clybourn Street, his wife and daughters did the cooking for the business, which also doubled as a restaurant.[285]

By the 1920s Italian women increasingly had independent roles in such endeavors. After traveling with her husband Frank when making purchases and doubling as his adviser, Mary Pastorino inherited the produce business in 1910 upon Frank's death and established her own tearoom after selling the produce business. Similarly, Anna DiMaggio ran a butcher shop after the death of her husband and performed "unfeminine" tasks such as preparing sausages. Of the forty women operating grocery stores in the Italian community between 1900 and 1930, eight were widows.[286] Though it was common for married women and widowed women in the Italian community to operate ethnic businesses upon the death of a husband or other relative, this was far from the extent of their involvement in the running of these stores.

There was also significant involvement by Italian women "whose contributions to a business enterprise have never been appreciated fully because they…worked alongside their husbands in family-owned businesses."[287] In addition to her grandmother and aunts working in her grandfather's tavern, Antoinette Carini's mother also kept track of credit at the store and deposited money in the bank for the business.[288] This practice was not unique in the Italian community as the books and banking transactions were maintained in the Catalanos' expanding produce business by the family matriarch.[289]

Stores run by women—either independently or indirectly—did not magically appear when Italian immigrants arrived to the United States,

Family Life in Milwaukee's Italian Community

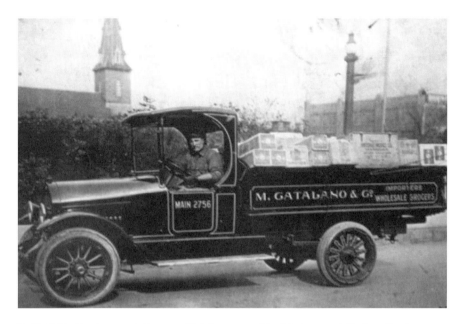

In 1916 M. Catalano and Co. was officially operated by Mariano and Cosimo Catalano. However, Mrs. Catalano performed many of the daily business operations. *Photo courtesy of the Italian Community Center of Milwaukee.*

though this practice did expand in American cities. Gaetano Balisteri's parents operated the only store in the town of Sant' Elia, Sicily, from which many Italian immigrants in Milwaukee emigrated. Though Gaetano's father was registered as the store owner, Gaetano's mother really ran the store while her husband made his living as a seasonal fisherman.[290]

This practice carried over to the United States as Gaetanina Balisteri's father worked as a coal miner during the day, while his wife operated a small grocery store within the community.[291] This pattern was almost identical to other Italian immigrants in Milwaukee. Antoinette Carini's father worked in the coal yards during the day, while his wife helped her parents run their tavern and restaurant.[292] Therefore, women were often the very face of the ethnic Italian stores that resonated so well with Italian immigrants in Milwaukee. In these ethnically Italian stores "generally women attended to the light business, while their husbands [were] at work on the tracks or in the foundries."[293] Though not officially recorded in city directories or other sources, Italian women were often front and center in the process of establishing an Italian cultural identity via their activities in these businesses.

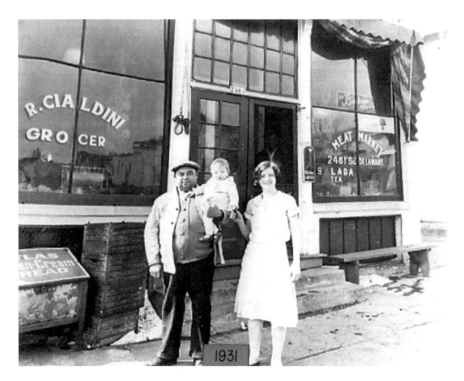

For women like Eleanora Cialdini, family space was also work space. Eleanora and her husband, Remigio, also lived at their Bay View store. *Photo courtesy of the Italian Community Center of Milwaukee.*

Italian-American women who ran businesses increasingly became independent. The businesses that Italian women owned themselves ranged from Jeanette Corti's ice cream parlor to Rose Maniaci's restaurant, the Canadian Club, to Catherine Dentice, who owned a fruit peddling business and then started her own grocery store. In Milwaukee, Italian women owned 40 of 130 Italian grocery stores between 1900 and 1930. Vecchio points out that all of these women had been born in Italy. The entrepreneurship of Milwaukee's Italian women far exceeded the national average for the presence of Italian-American women as merchants, which hovered around 7 percent.[294] The motivation for engaging in such pursuits lay in the fact that many Italian men served as seasonal workers, creating a need for additional income.[295] However, the nature of female work in Milwaukee was also closely tied to notions about gender and family roles.

As was often the case with Italian women involved in running grocery stores, employment was usually connected to domesticity. Historically, for the immigrant woman, "the combination of paid work with heavy domestic responsibilities has been the norm."[296] For example, in addition to working for The Alamo saloon as a bookkeeper and banker, Antoinette Carini's mother also found that as the oldest of fourteen children, "it was her duty…to take on the responsibility of raising the younger kids and cooking and things like that."[297] While younger Italian girls took on such additional responsibilities, some families split responsibilities in pursuit of the family economy. When an Italian mother of ten children died during the Great Depression, the oldest son dropped out of school at age fourteen to work for Western Union while the oldest sister took care of her younger siblings.[298]

To deal with the exceedingly diverse nature of Anna Torretta's family businesses, her daughter Josephine had to be taken out of school at age sixteen to run the Shorewood store located on Capitol and Downer.[299] Similarly, after the unexpected death of Gaetanina Balisteri's mother from childbirth in 1924 at the age of thirty-six, it was Gaetanina's sister who had to drop out of high school to help support the family by working at the family's grocery store and watching her younger siblings.[300] If viewed solely through American ideals, one may conclude the inherent conservative nature of the Italian family. However, many immigrants had left a country in which "very few Italian women knew how to read or write or even knew Latin," and where it was actually *illegal* in some communities to educate girls beyond comprehension of their own name. In nineteenth-century Italy, only certain females such as the mayor's daughter were able to pursue a solid education.[301]

Such deep-rooted practices in Italy were often combined with American conceptions of gender. American "feminine" ideals received an entire page in the *Italian Leader* in the 1930s and included tips on how to wash dishes, cook, apply mascara and be a good mother by doing the laundry.[302] The economic and educational experiences of Italian immigrants in Italy, along with American ideals of domesticity, led to confirmations about female domesticity and led to Italian girls supporting their families after a family tragedy or during extreme economic difficulties.

Italian familial ideals were also instrumental in influencing social structures. In Sicily, "peasant wives also continued to supervise their oldest daughters, training them for their later lives as housewives and mothers, working together with them until the daughters married."[303] After dropping out of school to run the family grocery store, Josephine Rampolla noted that her mother "kept me quite tied to her strings" until she married at the age of twenty-seven.[304] Likewise, Jennie Firmano did not marry until the age of

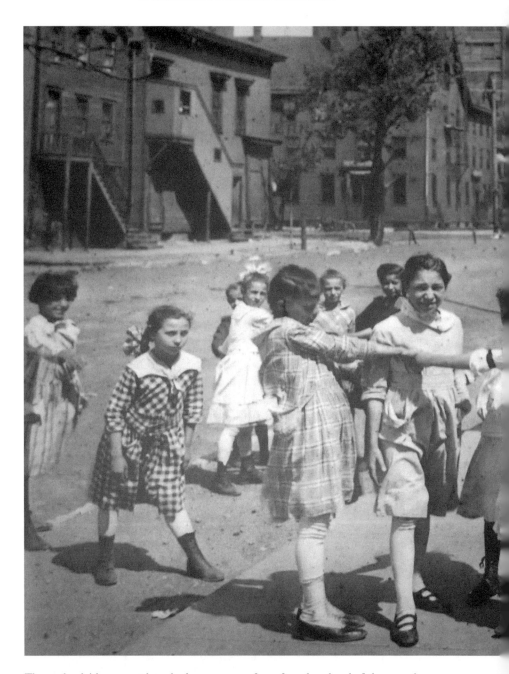

These schoolgirls may not have had many years of carefree play ahead of them, as the Great Depression forced teenage girls to take on additional responsibilities. *Photo courtesy of the Italian Community Center of Milwaukee.*

Family Life in Milwaukee's Italian Community

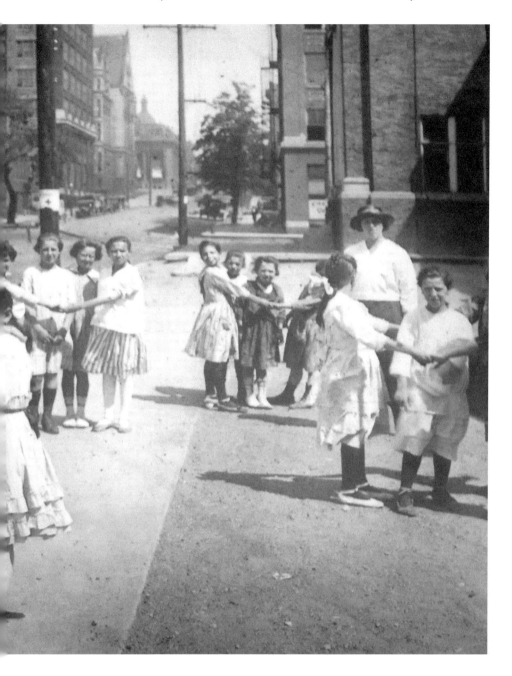

thirty-three, living at home during that time, citing her active role in running her barbershop.[305] As noted earlier, Italian-American women occasionally worked industrial jobs to supplement family income as well as often taking leading roles in small family businesses. However, despite their economic contributions to the family, many men "thought it was an insult to send a lady to work."[306] In addition to these economic ideals, Italian immigrants incorporated their beliefs on female education and very close familial ties to American life. Some of these attitudes carried over from Italy would be transformed in the 1920s and beyond, largely along generational lines.

Show Us the Money: Home Work and Paid Labor

Though many Italian women found work in family businesses, there were also Italian women in Milwaukee who worked as paid laborers, just not as often as in other American cities. Occasionally, women would obtain seamstress jobs at companies such as Adler's by utilizing skills learned in Italy such as finishing coats.[307] Some Italian-American women such as Josephine Rampolla's older sisters found work to supplement family income in Milwaukee at the Princess Candy Factory in the Third Ward.[308] The Princess Candy Factory allowed young girls to work within the Third Ward and pursue traditionally female professions. Such jobs were not common in Milwaukee, as the city's economy was based upon heavy manufacturing and often did not attract married women. It entailed a fifty-four- to sixty-hour workweek, with upward of eighty-five- to ninety-hour workweeks during peak periods.[309] Though precise income amounts for these jobs are difficult to determine in Milwaukee, comparable work, such as women working in macaroni factories in Chicago in the 1910s, paid approximately four to five dollars per week.[310]

The presence of immigrant women in the workforce was both an expression of "feminine" work as well as a contradiction of traditional American ideals. Men overwhelmingly worked as manual laborers in "masculine" jobs that entailed great physical danger, and many Italian men suffered from work-related illnesses and deaths.[311] However, Italian women also faced work-related dangers, as one Italian girl died as the result of a gasoline accident.[312] Catastrophic industrial tragedies such as the 1911 Triangle Shirtwaist Factory fire in New York City, which killed over 140 Russian Jews and Italians, eventually led to greater safety standards. Yet, Americans also complained about the "moral dangers" of women in the workforce, such as increased flirting between men and women and the association of immigrant women with prostitution.[313] While Italian women found paid work in the 1910s and 1920s at much lower rates than Italian men, more women from the second generation of Italian-American immigrants found work in the 1930s during the Great Depression.

A Second-Generation Workforce

The stagnant state of the American economy in the 1930s, along with the desire among second-generation Italians in Milwaukee to better their conditions financially, contributed to a rise in female employment in the community, though old attitudes toward female work sometimes remained. After attending Spencer College, Mary Busalacchi was made the first bursar of Marquette University in 1924.[314] Mary Sorgi also became very successful as a seasonal employee for Gimbels department store in 1938. Eventually, she became the top seller in the entire Midwest and found her knowledge of Italian very useful when making purchases overseas. Mary's professional success did not mean an abandonment of Italian customs, however; her mother helped raise her children and her husband worked as a police detective in the city.[315] Still, such success outside the ethnic Italian neighborhoods and community was by no means common, and more often, women became involved in traditionally female professions.

Women's roles in the family economy expanded in innovative ways as tough economic times saw male laborers laid off. During the Great Depression after her father was laid off from the coal yards, Antoinette Carini recalled that her

> mom had a little piece of land in the back of the house which would have been our backyard. She, as I said, was very aggressive. She turned it into a parking lot because of the fact that we had the post office two blocks away, and then we had Northwestern Mutual a block away. She then started this little parking lot, and that's how she made some money to be able to feed the family.[316]

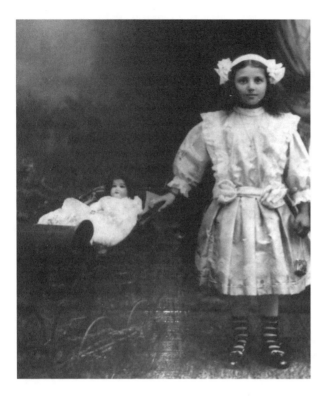

Rose Fricano Carini, circa 1910. *Photo courtesy of the Italian Community Center of Milwaukee.*

Irene Bertoglio worked as a seamstress for Gimbels and changed traditional "homework" activities into paid labor.[317] Other women also helped to make ends meet during the Depression by working part time as seamstresses for manufacturers such as Brill's Manufacturing Company on Water Street.[318] The second generation of Milwaukee's Italians that grew up during the Depression utilized skills like sewing, learned in their Italian neighborhoods, to work in the city, creating unique ways to help their families through difficult times.

Historian Donna Gabaccia has noted that during the Depression, there was a movement within immigrant communities to encourage young women to seek white-collar jobs like clerical work due to lower rates of unemployment in that sector and to more fully encourage female education.[319] In Milwaukee, Anna Ramponi's work as a typist for Cutler-Hammer, Inc., exemplified this trend.[320] The increasing presence of Italian women in white-collar jobs offered increased opportunities for Italian females outside of ethnic communities. However, this change was not universal, and conflicts over the position of women in the community would sometimes create heated debates, particularly among generational lines in the Italian community.

SOCIAL ROLES

The dramatically different work environments between Italy and the United States had a significant impact on changing gender roles in Milwaukee's Italian community. Though the Sicilian ideals discussed earlier sought to have males in charge of the family economy and females caring for the children and domestic duties, it was often not the reality in Italy. About 75 percent of Milwaukee's first-generation Italians had been *contadini* (farmers) or *pescatori* (fishermen) in Italy, typically engaged in seasonal work requiring long travel distances. In Milwaukee, Italian men working as fruit peddlers, garbage collectors and railroad workers could spend much more time with their families.[321] Many of these unskilled jobs were located within or nearby the Italian neighborhoods in the Third Ward or Bay View. Similar to New York's Italian community, this proximity to work created more of a domestic emphasis for women.[322] While Italian women were often actively involved in ethnic businesses, they were also expected to take on new social and domestic responsibilities, which created both opportunities and constraints upon the women in the community.

The opportunities that changing gender roles presented to Italian women often took place in the social sphere. The most common new opportunity for Italian women and girls was translation. Most commonly, teenage Italian girls with some knowledge of English were paid by older immigrants to serve as interpreters during family illnesses and to translate American naturalization papers.[323] Due to the fact that "most of these people did not speak much English at the time," there was a void in the community for a mediator to facilitate communication between Italian-speaking immigrants and the larger city as a whole.[324] Sometimes, this tension centered on legal issues: "Milwaukee's Italians were often jailed for carrying concealed weapons or for violating a city ordinance."[325] To fill this void, a woman named Carlotta served as an interpreter of sorts for the community. When "Italian families… had any problem with the City Hall, their license or something, or they were in any trouble, they would go to Carlotta."[326] Lizzie Ritagliatto in the Third Ward was paid by Brett Funeral Home in 1901 to bring doctors to sick immigrants and inform the funeral home of a death in the family.[327] Italian girls successfully mediated relations between the Italian community and the city, indicative of the other social roles that they successfully fulfilled.

The continuing feature of Milwaukee's Italian community as an international community connected by heavy rates of return migration also created other social voids. Therefore, in addition to raising six children

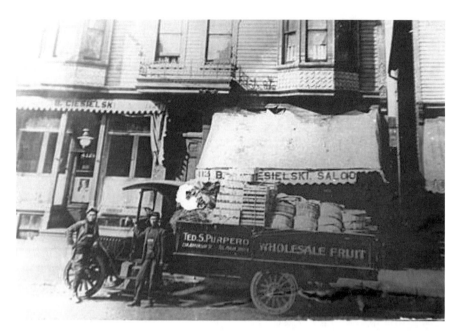

Italian men like Ted and Carl Purpero played larger roles in family life in Milwaukee than in Italy because they could work close to home. *Photo courtesy of the Italian Community Center of Milwaukee.*

of her own, "many men who had come to the city without their families" came to Mary Busalacchi, who aided their adjustment to American life.[328] Though the exact reasons for the visible presence of individuals such as Mary Busalacchi and Carlotta are not clear, it is possible that Italian-American men viewed the interpreter role as fulfilling some type of necessary bridge between the private community and the public. While these roles may seem somewhat trivial, they were not to Italian immigrants, as it was believed that the more extensive a family's network of friends, the greater that family would be respected by others in the community as it was a form of social capital.[329] Through cooperation, Italian families believed that they would be able to enhance not only their individual family's prestige, but the reputation of the Italian community as a whole.

Just as initial language barriers created opportunities for Italian women as interpreters, religious life was also tied to femininity in Milwaukee's Italian community. Italian women were deemed to be religious guardians, and the congregation at church services was composed almost entirely of women and children.[330] Italian women in Pompeii's religious community developed a strong attachment to the church's namesake and common figure of Catholic veneration: Mary, the mother of Jesus. According to Italian Community Center historian Mario Carini, religious devotions to Mary "provided a perfectly plausible and pious reason for a woman to escape from her grueling household responsibilities and socialize with her long-suffering sisters."[331]

The men who did attend in the first generation of Italian immigrants often stood in the back or just outside Pompeii Church and talked among themselves, as was the tradition in late nineteenth-century Italy.[332] Instead, the religious involvement of men in the community was concerned with the patron saint of their village of origin and focused on the *feste* that will be discussed in chapter five.[333] Among first-generation Italian immigrants in Milwaukee, religious activities attracted more women and children both numerically and symbolically, and resulted in the role of the Italian mother as the person in charge of religious observance in the family.[334] "As the Italians began the long climb into the middle class," Italian men in the 1920s and 1930s built upon the efforts by first-generation Italian women, and "their attitude toward the Church shifted from casual attachment to fierce identification."[335]

The linkage of religion to Italian women was not the only aspect of an expanded Italian cultural identity in the 1920s and 1930s. In 1905 Italian fraternal organizations were only open to men "who had been either born in the Italian hometown" of a particular society or the son of an immigrant from the sponsoring society's village.[336] Therefore, the exclusive framework of these societies reaffirmed a regional identity while also excluding a large segment of the community. However, historian Donna Gabaccia argues that "within ten to twenty years of a fraternal's foundation, immigrant men would abandon exclusionary practices to welcome women as auxiliary members."[337]

In contrast to earlier ethnic organizations in Milwaukee, the 1933 incorporation of the Casa Italiana cited "the improvement of the spiritual, mental, social, and physical conditions *of the men and women*" as its major goal within the Italian community.[338] Rather than being peripheral participants, Italian women such as Anita Sorgi joined organizations such as the Italian Civic Association and worked toward the creation of an Italian community center in 1933.[339] Therefore, it can be concluded that immigrant women shifted the fraternal focus from "male sociability and breadwinning into organizations dedicated to the creation and reproduction of ethnicity."[340] Expansions of Italian culture in the 1920s and 1930s coincided with broader cultural and political movements that will be discussed in chapter five.

Marriage and Dating

Among first-generation Italians in Milwaukee, marriages were typically arranged by the parents of the boy and girl as had often been done in Italy.[341] Though a historian noted that in 1945, "the children had little to say about the marriage match," an examination of oral histories reveals this was not always true.[342] After receiving an offer of marriage from Antonio Balisteri of Milwaukee, Mariano Alioto of Denver shared the news with his daughter, who had already received five other offers. She then proceeded to select Antonio and the two were married in 1908 and moved to Milwaukee. In other words, arranged marriages were common, though women sometimes had some say in the manner among first-generation Italians.[343] Some of the increased independence for young Italians can be explained by return migration.

Like almost every other aspect of life, marriage patterns among Italians were transformed by return migration. After returning to Italy from the Americas, men from central Italy increasingly began to serenade lovers by the 1890s in the pursuit of romantic love as a challenge to traditional arranged marriages.[344] Likewise, young men who had yet to travel to the Americas were viewed as less desirable potential husbands than migrants who had been to the Americas.[345] Italian return migration thus contributed to changing courtship practices on both sides of the Atlantic.

Whereas first-generation Italians, especially girls, married in their teens, courtship and marriage habits began to change in the 1930s and 1940s. Overwhelmingly, Italians married fellow Italians in the first generation, often from the same town of origin. However, Joe DiMaggio, whose butcher shop was mentioned earlier, married a Jewish woman, Angeline, and worked closely with her in the store.[346] As of 1930, they both were working for the butcher shop, and she took over the shop upon Joe's passing.[347] From 1936 onward, it was common for Italian boys living in the Third Ward to have steady Polish girlfriends from the South Side in addition to Italian girlfriends from their neighborhood.[348]

The expansion of popular culture activities in the 1930s also changed dating practices. Italian *feste* provided teenagers new opportunities to flirt and go on dates. Outside of the Italian neighborhoods, second-generation Italians would travel in groups to McKinley Beach or to dance clubs where some Italians, such as Anthony Dicristo, met their future spouses.[349] Younger Italians also would play baseball together in the Third Ward, and some went to downtown Milwaukee's Pabst Theater and the Blatz Beer Gardens with their parents.[350] Other Italians went to the Pabst and Majestic Theaters to enhance their English skills.[351] Other Italians took advantage of their proximity to downtown and went shopping or perused the Milwaukee Public Library.[352] When teenagers went on dates, Italian girls often took friends or family members along to act as chaperones.[353]

Inter-ethnic marriages became much more pronounced in the 1940s. Ann Maniscalco's marriage to Nickolas Romano in 1947 was the solitary instance of twelve Maniscalco children to marry another Italian.[354] While major changes regarding intermarriage and courtship were affected by the sprawl of Italians throughout Milwaukee, another factor was the close scrutiny under which Italian families kept their daughters.

The experiences of women in Milwaukee's Italian-American neighborhoods and communities were both liberating yet also constraining, sometimes painfully so. Despite obtaining a college degree in 1939, one resident's older sister was only able to pursue a teaching position after obtaining the consent of her father to do so. Her father was persuaded following the intervention of her other siblings who convinced their father to reconsider.[355] After obtaining her college degree in the 1940s from Marquette University and considering law school, an Italian woman was told by her prospective husband that he wanted to "know if I wanted to be a lawyer" or a wife.[356]

Controversial Claims: Rapes and Lynchings

It was viewed as the obligation of the father in Sicily to monitor his wife and daughter closely, but this often did not become a reality as Italian men rarely were in town more than a day or two during harvest times. However, in the United States, men took a much more active role in family affairs. In 1915 and 1916 a thirteen-year-old Italian girl was raped repeatedly, resulting in the birth of a child and another child that was born the year after, but died shortly thereafter. To avoid retribution by other Italian men in the community, the perpetrator was sent back to Italy, and the now fourteen-year-old girl, at the behest of her parents, married a thirty-seven-year-old man to save face.[357] When perpetrators did not leave the country, they were met with the harshest of penalties.

According to a former Third Ward resident, in 1930 "a black man raped an Italian girl in the Third Ward, and the padrones hanged him." When police in the city tried to stop the lynching, segments of the Milwaukee mob wielded machine guns, forcing the police to leave. The same former resident also recalled that "an Italian man raped an Italian girl too. Twenty-five cops came to get the fellow. The padrones fired their warning shots with the machine-guns again and told the cops, 'Get the hell out of here, we'll take care of it.'" Upon which time, they strung the Italian man up on a pole and broke his neck.[358] Though unable to verify with newspaper accounts, these instances illustrate the importance to Milwaukee's early Italian community of monitoring certain deviant behaviors.

Conclusion

In Italy, it was common for Italian women to run domestic tasks and also be responsible for social connections, while Italian men often worked away from home and were not present due to work requirements. Educationally, Italian women were at a distinct disadvantage, as Italian families discouraged education and instead tried to implement domestic skills such as sewing, which had the potential to boost the family income. The ideals of Italians and American assumptions about women being dependents without examination contributed to changes in gender roles. Equally important was the fact that Italian men worked much more closely to their houses and took a much more active interest in family affairs.

In past historical accounts, Italian immigrant women have been characterized as housewives with few other responsibilities. However, this is an extremely inaccurate historical picture to paint. While Italian women in Milwaukee were not employed at the same levels as Italian men due to Milwaukee's economic focus on heavy industry, Italian women played integral functions in ethnic businesses such as grocery stores. Though not always paid or fully documented, Italian-American women performed duties essential to the well-being of the family. In addition to serving important roles in ethnic businesses, Italian women did obtain work in light industries and also performed home work, which added to the family income using traditional women's trades such as sewing. The 1930s saw an increase, though not a complete turnaround, in attitudes about white-collar employment for women and increased levels of education as second-generation Italians were typically more able to pursue a middle-class lifestyle than their parents had been.

Family Life in Milwaukee's Italian Community

Occupational patterns along with regional identities greatly shaped the experience of Italian immigrants. The extremely high composition of Italian emigrant males made it much more likely that they envisioned life in the Americas as temporary until they were reunited with their wives and children in Italy.[359] When viewed globally, the overwhelming historical evidence and extent of return migration contradicts "the ideology of American exceptionalism…that every person who set foot on American soil believed himself so fortunate that returning to the native country was unthinkable."[360]

In economic terms, the prevalence of Italian women actively involved in running grocery stores and other ethnic businesses sometimes gave Italian women the wherewithal to establish their own businesses. As one of seven children born to Sicilian immigrants, Jennie Firmano owned and operated her own barbershop from 1938 to 1969.[361] Similarly, Josephine Rampolla, whose mother took her out of school to run the family grocery store, established her own business in 1966 and ran it until selling it in 1986.[362]

Italian women not employed as paid laborers played crucial roles in the community by serving as interpreters and bridging the gap between older Italians and the larger "outside" world of Milwaukee. This prestigious Italian role was made all the more relevant as return migration continued to increase until 1910 and led to many Italian males arriving in Milwaukee without families. Religiously, Italian women were more active in weekly church services than Italian men and were expected to pass this on to their children. In terms of marriage, Italian girls often married in their teens and had their future husbands chosen for them by their parents, though this practice decreased sharply by the 1930s.

Milwaukee's Italian women experienced expanded economic influence compared to Italy, while experiencing mixed social fortunes that continually emphasized domesticity. Chapter five will explore popular culture and religious celebrations in the Italian community, the development of an Italian-American identity in the 1930s, the reaction of the community to the rise of Mussolini and the impact of World War II upon Milwaukee's Italian-American community.

CHAPTER 5

CULTURAL DEVELOPMENT AMID INTERNATIONAL CRISES, 1899–1945

Oswaldo Natarelli's father worked in the United States between 1920 and 1928 while his wife and son stayed in Italy until enough money could be saved for their passage. The mother and son lived in fear in Abruzzo and witnessed a woman spitting off a balcony where, unknown to her, a Fascist parade was taking place. Charged with dishonoring the Italian flag, the woman was shackled with chains and arrested.[363] Oswaldo's mother was also disturbed by the presence of the *ballila*, or Mussolini's Youth Movement, and refused to let her son join since she wanted to keep him out of future military obligations.[364] Similar resentment of the Fascist regime could also be found in a former boat laborer who was considered to be a Socialist by the Fascists since he was part of a union. After having his hours cut by the Fascists, Phillip Firmano emigrated from Italy to work in Waukegan, Illinois, in 1923 and then to Milwaukee in 1924 to work in tanneries.[365]

In Milwaukee, Italian cultural and religious celebrations—known individually as a *festa* or collectively as *feste*—emphasized the continuing influence of a regional identity and world view between 1899 and 1908, but became more "Italian" in the 1920s and 1930s. The impact of a greater Italian identity was also evident in ethnic newspaper accounts, the reception of Italian consuls and expressions of American nationalism after World War I. Coinciding with national and local anti-immigrant sentiment, Italians rallied behind various efforts and organizations in defense of this emerging identity. Partially in response to the 1917 involvement of Italian anarchist activities, non-Italians in Milwaukee became suspicious of expressions of

Italian nationalism in Bay View, while generally enjoying wider acceptance in the Third Ward. In the 1930s, celebrations in the Third Ward were attended by many non-Italians and replicated in smaller communities such as Waukesha.

Almost simultaneously, Benito Mussolini was remaking Italy into a Fascist, authoritarian state, causing some cleavages within the community. To counter American claims of inferiority, some Milwaukee Italians supported Mussolini in his quest to transform Italy into a more influential world power. Others questioned supporting a country to which they were ideologically opposed and had voluntarily left for economic and political reasons. Among non-Italians in the United States, Mussolini was admired for his opposition to communism but drew skepticism after the invasion of Ethiopia in 1935.

Once the United States entered World War II, the participation of Milwaukee's Italians via the United States' military service, fundraising efforts and war production further emphasized this American political association. The nature of the war, including the invasion of Sicily in 1943, caused concern for the safety of relatives still in Italy and also led to humanitarian efforts. The end of World War II in 1945 also marked the end of an almost fifty-year period in which the Italian state had a periodic yet significant impact on Milwaukee's Italian community. While the political relevance was largely curtailed, the cultural legacy of Milwaukee's Italian community was preserved.

MILWAUKEE'S *FESTE*, 1899–1908

Whereas the Italian-American community in Milwaukee experienced differences in terms of economics, housing, places of origin and gender roles, religious associations were closely tied to social activities within the community. Italian immigrants were overwhelmingly Catholic and typically decided to settle in cities and neighborhoods already populated by their relatives, both of which represented their determination to maintain cultural ties to their homeland.[366] However, while maintaining these cultural ties often meant settling near the largest Italian Catholic Church, Our Lady of Pompeii on 419 North Jackson Street, it also caused tensions over the nature of the church. As mentioned in chapter two, there was an outcry within the Italian community over the placement of a northern Italian

Cultural Development Amid International Crises, 1899–1945

priest in the predominantly Sicilian Third Ward. The emphasis on having a Sicilian religious leader within the community contributed to the broader characteristic of the Third Ward as a strongly Sicilian neighborhood.

Following the dispute over Italian priests, the church did play an essential role in bringing the Third Ward's Italian immigrant population together. In particular, Our Lady of Pompeii "was the focal point" of the neighborhood in which over half of all weddings were held.[367] But it is interesting to note that one Italian joined the Seventh-Day Adventist Church not only on religious grounds, but also due to the fact that he did not drink or smoke.[368] Though seemingly an anomaly, it is further confirmation of the Church's overtly social role for Italian immigrants.

As has been discussed in previous chapters, Italian immigrants did not necessarily identify themselves as "Italians" per se, but rather as former residents of a particular town or region of Italy. This legacy from the mixed results of Italian unification discussed in chapter one had a lasting impact upon the Italian community in Milwaukee. Some of Milwaukee's Italian immigrants emigrated from the fishing village of Porticello, Sicily, and like many towns in Sicily, had their own patron saint. For Porticello, the patron saint was *Madonna del Lume*, or the Blessed Mother of Light, around whom Italian immigrants in Milwaukee founded a mutual aid society, *Madonna del Lume*.[369] The custom of having patron saints and forming mutual aid societies around them revealed not only the religious inclinations of Milwaukee's Italians, but also their conceptions of maintaining ties to their village of origin.

While some Sicilian towns had Mary as a patron saint, other Sicilian immigrants had Joseph as the patron saint of their hometown. In March 1899, the *Catholic Citizen* remarked that:

> *the feast of St. Joseph was celebrated with much devotion and rejoicing, in their own peculiar manner, by the Italian colony of Milwaukee. It was a three day celebration beginning Sunday with religious services and followed by other rejoicings until Tuesday night. Altars were erected at the houses of Frank Olongi, Nic DeGeorgie, Joseph Burgerino, and Tony Macalus, all located in the lower Third Ward. Many beautiful offerings were laid at the shrine of the great saint. The central altar piece consisted of a fine picture of St. Joseph, profusely wreathed in ferns and evergreens, brilliantly illuminated with lamps and candles. Leading up in terraced rows before the statue were offerings after the Italian custom, of fruits, wines, olives, macaroni, fancy breads, cakes, confections, sfinge and pignoista—the latter*

a dish made of eggs and flour fried in honey is the delight of Italian epicures. Overhead was stretched a canopy draped with silk handkerchiefs, ribbons, laces and covers, the walls being tapestried with the same.[370]

Celebrations such as this feast in 1899 celebrated the residents' hometown and would expand over time to include the Italian community as a whole.

The increased presence of Italian immigrants in the United States after 1900 was becoming clear to many Americans in religious and cultural terms. Religiously, newspapers such as the *Catholic Citizen* of Milwaukee frequently noted the discrepancy between the number of Italian immigrants entering the United States and the shortage of priests who spoke Italian.[371] In Milwaukee, there were efforts by non-Italian religious leaders such as Reverend David O'Hearn of St. John's Cathedral to connect with the Italian immigrants. Having studied in Italy and being fluent in Italian, O'Hearn had a strong affinity for Italian culture, so much so that visiting Italian composer Pietro Mascagni remarked that O'Hearn "could be taken for a born Roman."[372]

Despite efforts by O'Hearn and religious celebrations discussed above, Italian immigrants pushed to have their own church in which they would have a greater degree of independence over not only religious manners, but cultural celebrations as well.[373] Therefore, the arrival of an Italian priest, Rosario Nasca, was met very favorably by the Italian community, and Nasca headed an Italian mission, or small chapel, that was affiliated with St. John's Cathedral, but was located in the Third Ward on 180 Huron Street and catered to the Italian community.[374] Such an arrangement was a precursor to the establishment of an Italian church and more frequent Italian cultural expressions.

The push for an Italian church accelerated after 1900, when fundraising efforts drew support from prominent non-Italian Catholics in Milwaukee such as Thomas Neacy, Judge Paul Carpenter and cookie manufacturer Robert Johnson, who personally donated $6,000 in 1902.[375] When Milwaukee's Italian immigrants had obtained enough finances, they purchased a lot in 1902 and called the church *Madonna di Pompeii*, or Blessed Virgin of Pompeii.[376] Then, after the 1903 controversy over the northern origins of Joseph Angeletti and more fundraising efforts, both northern and southern Italians built the church and laid the cornerstone in October 1904.[377] The creation of an Italian parish in Milwaukee was not an easy task nor without in-fighting, but it was made possible through the efforts of Italians in Milwaukee to have their own parish, as well as the financial contributions of non-Italians in the city.

Cultural Development Amid International Crises, 1899–1945

In Italy, there was often a lack of established institutions and as a result, many Italian towns developed their own unique customs and carved out their own niches independent of both the Italian state as well as the Catholic Church.[378] In particular, southern Italy had a large amount of autonomy through *ricettizie* churches, in which local priests ran parishes in rural communities, largely independent of the Vatican. This long tradition of self-rule in southern Italy lasted for centuries and as recently as 1850, 74 percent of parish churches in Puglia and 94 percent of churches from Basilicata were *ricettizie* churches.[379]

This traditional autonomy within churches was carried over to Milwaukee and contributed to a sense of ownership in religious matters. Immigrants from the Sicilian town of Santo Stefano di Camastra, the *Stefnari*, came to Milwaukee in large numbers in the 1890s and formed a mutual aid society, which carried on their hometown's tradition of having a festival in honor of the patron saint of their village in Italy. After obtaining permission from the City of Milwaukee and the Catholic Church, the *Festa Alla Santissima Santa Croce* was held on September 15–16, 1906, in the Third Ward near the new Pompeii Church. In a scene reminiscent of the 1899 celebration, Italians in the Third Ward celebrated with live music, Italian cuisine, Italian attire and dances, as well as fireworks and a religious procession.[380] The 1899 celebrations were described by Milwaukeeans simply as "peculiar," but there was a backlash against cultural celebrations in other American cities.

Just a few months after Milwaukee's Italian *festa* was held in September, a strong pronouncement against such events was made by Catholic authorities in Rome. In a December 1906 message to New York, reporters in Rome noted,

> *Frequent complaints have reached here from American priests and bishops that southern Italians residing in the United States continue to celebrate the feasts of their patron saints "mure Italico," in the same manner they used to do in their native towns in Italy with street parades, illuminations, fireworks and other features which, the complainants intimate, are not only wholly unnecessary, but positively objectionable to Catholics and non-Catholics alike in America, because of a different conception of religion prevailing in that country.*[381]

While American religious figures found Italian *feste* to be "objectionable" and "unnecessary," the celebrations were an expression of their ties to Italy, as well as to the practice established in Italian artisan guilds of sponsoring

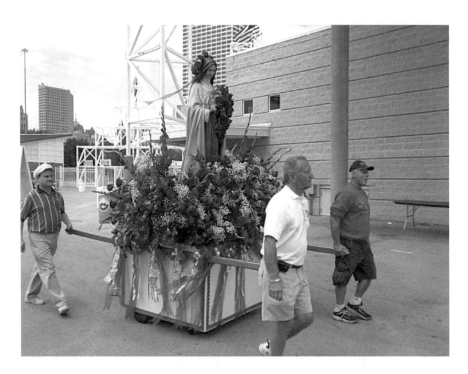

Religious processions, like this one honoring Mary at Festa Italiana 2009, have been focal points for Milwaukee *feste* for more than one hundred years. *Photo by Cindy Zignego.*

feste to honor both the patron saint as well as "honest workers" in the community.[382] Unsympathetic to these issues, Vatican authorities ordered American bishops "that measures be adopted for the gradual suppression of similar southern Italian customs." However, the Vatican also noted that American bishops should proceed with caution since Italians had rioted and protested against Church authorities in the past when they tried to put an end to such celebrations.[383]

In Milwaukee, archbishop Sebastian Messmer banned the parish priest from taking part in *feste*, only to have the Italian community find a different priest to lead the procession and borrow statues from a statue store rather than from the church.[384] Rather than being accepted by American and Vatican religious authorities, Italian *feste* were initially deemed unusual, dangerous and unorthodox but were maintained by Italians.

Such anecdotes reflect the very deep tensions between the Italian state and the Catholic Church, which occurred for over fifty years following Italian annexation of the papal states in the 1870s and generally fall

Cultural Development Amid International Crises, 1899–1945

outside the scope of this book. However, the Catholic Church as well as the Italian state took an active interest in emigrants abroad. While Italian reformers urged emigrants to think of themselves as both Catholics and Italians, Italian immigrants in the United States would develop their own Italian identity along cultural lines, largely on their own terms. While host countries such as the United States viewed Catholic missionaries more favorably than the involvement of the Italian state, due to a Catholic push for more assimilation generally, the heavy-handedness of efforts to crack down on *feste* convinced Italian emigrants to pursue both cultural and religious connections to Italy—but do so on their own terms.[385]

Despite criticisms that their public displays and celebrations were unusual, Italians in Milwaukee continued to hold *feste*. Though a precise number is difficult to pin down based on oral history accounts, LeRoy Bertocini claimed that there were "at least three festivals a year."[386] When these *feste* were held, they were sponsored by religious societies and associations and "featured food, music, processions, and ear-splitting fireworks."[387] *Feste* typically were one to two blocks long and were "set in front of the old Pompeii Church."[388] The role of *feste* and other celebrations within the Italian-American community were also impacted and observed by non-Italians.

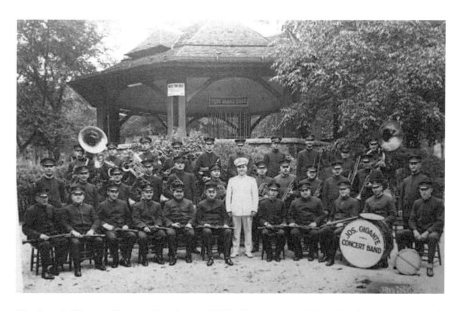

The Joseph Gigante Concert Band, circa 1925. *Photo courtesy of the Italian Community Center of Milwaukee.*

In 1908 a Milwaukee newspaper noted that the feast of the Holy Cross was held "by the Italians with a blithesomeness that seems odd to Catholics in this country." Like previous and future *feste*, the 1908 celebration had an Italian band that paraded through the Third Ward along with booths where Italians could purchase Italian desserts. Interestingly, both Italian and American flags were on display, and Milwaukee Mayor David Rose gave a speech on the second day of the festival.[389] Ironically, Italian religious celebrations such as *feste* would over the years become very closely tied to the celebration of Italian culture and traditions as well as Italian religion. The presence of an American flag at the 1908 *festa* was a fitting symbol for Italian popular celebrations and reflected a greater interest in American affairs by Italians in Milwaukee.

Americanization Pressures

As the Italian presence in Milwaukee became more pronounced, greater efforts were made by non-Italians as well as some Italians to assimilate the community to American standards. Just as chapters one and two discussed attempts by the Italian government to create a "Greater Italy" along cultural grounds, American institutions and the public responded in a variety of ways to instill Americanization among Italian immigrants. In response, the Italian community modified certain public displays while fiercely holding onto others.

Initially, the rapid self-reliance and traditional suspicion of authorities by Italian immigrants was apparent in their attitudes toward political figures, whether they were Italian or not. For example, when new Italian consular agent Armenio Conte arrived in Milwaukee in 1907, only 200 Italians of the 5,000 living in Milwaukee greeted him at the Northwestern railroad station.[390] Despite the lukewarm reception, the Italian presence in southeastern Wisconsin began to respond more positively to Italian consuls. In nearby Racine, Italian representatives from Milwaukee and Chicago joined Racine's leaders in emphasizing the importance of Italian history as well as American history. In the much smaller city, 250 Italians from southeastern Wisconsin enjoyed a meal made by an Italian chef, listened to an Italian band from Kenosha and saw an Italian flag unfurled next to an American flag donated by the Italian benevolent society.[391]

Cultural Development Amid International Crises, 1899–1945

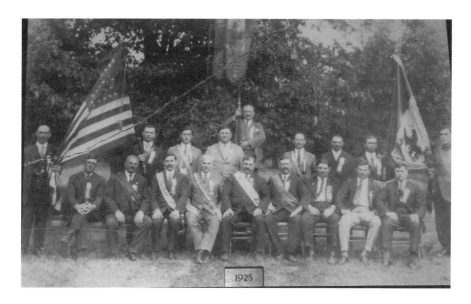

Fraternal organizations often celebrated both Italian and American identities. *Photo courtesy of the Italian Community Center of Milwaukee.*

In a gesture that became common in subsequent years, Angelo Cerminara, then secretary to consul Conte, spoke of the sacrifices made by American veterans who made it possible for Italian immigrants to pursue freedom.[392] The theme of Americanization was also pressed upon by Racine Mayor A. J. Horlick, who urged the Italian immigrants in the crowd to become educated about American politics and to process citizenship papers. He was greeted by enthusiastic cheers from the assembled crowd.[393] The flag dedication in Racine showcased efforts to establish an American political identity while maintaining an Italian cultural identity.

In 1912 the city of Milwaukee opened the Detroit School social center in the Italian neighborhood in the Third Ward. The social center became very popular, as it offered academic programs that assisted immigrants in learning English as well as hiring Italian immigrants to teach embroidering and other crafts to Milwaukeeans. On Saturday afternoons, the center was packed with Italian immigrants, and parents and children alike watched American movies. Prior to the start of the movie, "the social center's director Mr. Stivers, would ask the children to rise and give the Pledge of Allegiance."[394] This heavy focus on Americanization was typical of other social centers in Milwaukee between 1911 and 1920 as H.O. Berg, the director of the social centers, ordered their focus to be on assimilation.[395]

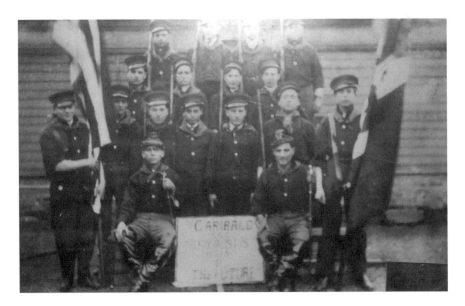

Italian Socialists in Milwaukee, 1918. The sign reads, "Garibaldi said the Socialists are the sun of the future." *Photo courtesy of the Italian Community Center of Milwaukee.*

As World War I erupted, popular celebrations were further pressured to have overt pro-American tones.

The participation of Italians during World War I would not be complete without discussing the role of Italian anarchists in 1917. After his failed attempts to convert Italians in the Third Ward and Bay View were met with much resistance and defense of Italian religious practices, Protestant Evangelist Reverend August Giuliani continued to seek new supporters. He also began to preach about the need for Italians in Milwaukee to support the American war effort. In September 1917, he was met by Italian opponents and a street fight ensued in Bay View involving Giuliani's followers, anarchists and Milwaukee police officers that killed two Italians and wounded two police officers. In November 1917, a bomb exploded at police headquarters in Milwaukee that killed ten people and caused outrage in Milwaukee as well as nationally. The bomb was linked to the confrontation between anti-war "anarchists" and Giuliani's supporters a few months earlier. While some police officers pushed Milwaukee to round up Italians in Bay View and the Third Ward, the lack of evidence for the bomb's perpetrators prevented Milwaukee Mayor Daniel Hoan from agreeing to this approach.[396]

The significance of this incident lay in its long-term as well as short-term results. Within the Italian community, such confrontations demonstrated

Cultural Development Amid International Crises, 1899–1945

the cleavages between more moderate Italian-Americans and radicals. The reaction to the 1917 bombing also revealed the growing anti-immigrant sentiment in the United States by nativists and the desire to "Americanize" them. Finally, these events cemented the notion in Bay View that Italians were "radicals" and would lead to future hostility to Italian displays of nationalism in that community.

A flier from the July 4, 1918 celebrations at Juneau Park showcased the active participation of Italian children in Independence Day activities. Though no Italians are mentioned by name, the Detroit Street School to which many Italian children went had an extremely active role in the festivities. Girls from the school participated in flag drills and recited the Pledge of Allegiance, and over 150 children sang American patriotic songs such as "The Star-Spangled Banner" and "Battle Hymn of the Republic."[397] Italian-American adults also could become caught up in the patriotic fervor that swept the United States during and shortly after World War I. On Armistice Day in 1918, there was a parade in which patrons in the Third Ward produced a "makeshift wagon" containing a dummy inside of a coffin "that was supposed to be the Kaiser."[398]

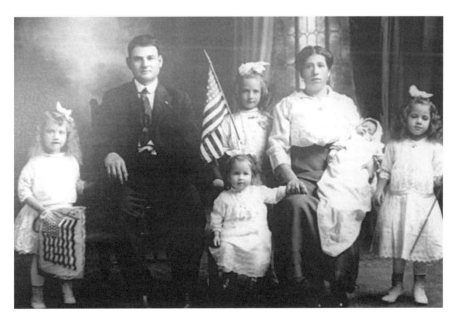

Italian-American families were anxious to prove their loyalties to the United States after the Italian anarchist violence in 1917. *Photo courtesy of the Italian Community Center of Milwaukee.*

Ethnic Festivals in Milwaukee

These gestures to American nationalism were characteristic of a broader political movement in Milwaukee after World War I. According to historian Victor Greene, between 1910 and 1940 Milwaukee Progressives wanted to "feature and maintain cultural heterogeneity; on the other hand, they also sought to prepare the foreigners to live in America. Hence, in a sense, they wished to both 'foreignize' and Americanize the arrivals!"[399]

As mentioned in chapter three, Milwaukee Socialist Mayor Emil Seidel publically financed social centers starting in 1911. These programs remained extremely popular and even expanded under the direction of Dorothy Enderis, who actively promoted cultural differences during her run as the director of the social centers from 1920 until 1948. In 1927 she and Milwaukee Mayor Daniel Hoan successfully lobbied the Wisconsin legislature to renew tax support for the social centers.[400]

In the 1920s and 1930s Milwaukee also regularly held public multiethnic festivals. In contrast, Buffalo rarely had multiethnic festivals, Detroit and Cleveland had festivals run by private organizers and Cincinnati's 1912 festival was held "to show that immigrants were really a social threat to the community needing immediate religious conversion."[401] Therefore, Milwaukee's publically financed and politically backed festivals were a rarity.[402]

A Taste of Milwaukee: 1920s and 1930s Celebrations

The 1920s witnessed an increased sense of Italian cultural belonging. In response to more restrictive immigration, as well as a desire to be more active in the larger Milwaukee and American communities and to hold onto cultural practices from Italy, public displays by Milwaukee's Italians increasingly incorporated both American and Italian themes. The growing Italian identity in Milwaukee expanded and differed from initial conceptions by Italian immigrants who emphasized their regional origins more commonly than claiming a common Italian background. The expansion of an Italian identity in Milwaukee was evident in public celebrations, Italian newspapers, growing interest in Italy's changing international status and increased contact between Milwaukee's Italian community and other Italian communities in southeastern Wisconsin.

Cultural Development Amid International Crises, 1899–1945

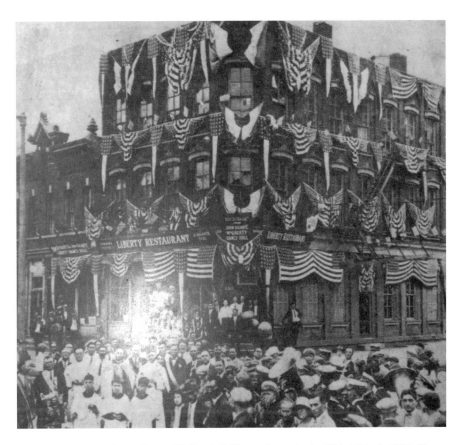

The John Gigante Liberty Dance Hall at 148 Huron Street in the Third Ward, 1925. *Photo courtesy of the Italian Community Center of Milwaukee.*

Eventually, Italian *feste* expanded to include several celebrations tied to a particular village's hometown. However, the festivals also became a celebration of being Italian and showcased the community's cultural dynamics. Celebrations such as the St. Joseph's *festa* in June 1925 included an Italian band, fireworks and a procession through the Third Ward. A photograph of the festival shows the Italian band alongside Italian men with tricolored sashes outside of the John Gigante Liberty Dance Hall on 148 Huron Street. One of the most striking things about the photo is that seven United States flags adorn the Liberty Restaurant in addition to numerous red, white and blue bunting decorating the façades of the three-story building.[403] Thus, for Italians in the Third Ward, such *feste* were celebrations of being both Italian and American.

The dramatic nature of *feste* and other parades within the Third Ward also drew the attention of fellow Milwaukeeans. According to Sam Purpero, in the 1920s and 1930s *feste* caused people to come to the Third Ward "from all over, non-Italians, non-Catholics…for that if you want to call it the taste of Milwaukee." Parking their cars on lawns within the neighborhood to catch a glimpse of fireworks, Milwaukeeans also were encouraged to buy food items from peddlers.[404] An array of culinary items such as hamburgers, sausages, cannoli and wine tantalized Milwaukeeans' taste buds, and an Italian band from Chicago pleased their ears outside of the Andrew Jackson school, across the street from Pompeii Church.[405]

Of particular interest to Italians was the Feast of San Giuseppe or St. Joseph since it was a religious celebration with a heavy culinary emphasis. With particular relevance to Milwaukee's unemployed Italians during the Great Depression, the March celebration was known as a day for alms giving as well as a day when everybody was to eat abundantly such traditional Italian cuisine as sliced oranges, rice, "baccala" or salted cod, artichokes, tomato sauce, fruit, cauliflower and cannoli—"all liberally accompanied by wine."[406] While the Feast of St. Joseph was celebrated within the family in Sicily, it was greatly expanded when adapted to American life. The 1934 St. Joseph *festa* marked the twenty-second year of celebration and was a two-day celebration in July that featured a concert performance by an Italian band and two fireworks displays culminating "with the famous Third Ward noisy fireworks, which are the talk of the town."[407] One of the main architects of the Third Ward's fireworks display was Sam Bartolotta, who as a second-generation Italian immigrant tried to re-create the Sicilian tradition of honoring a patron saint with a fireworks display.[408]

Unlike other American cities, Milwaukee actively promoted its cultural diversity while simultaneously encouraging Americanization. A 1928 effort by the *Milwaukee Journal* to profile different groups led them to characterize Italians as being temperamental but also "honest and thrifty," possessing strong family ties, and gave "color to their ward."[409] While many non-Italians had a love for the visual and culinary experiences of Italian *feste* in Milwaukee, one Third Ward resident wrote to Milwaukee Archbishop Stritch that the final night's fireworks display "resembled a battlefront and made night hideous for everyone."[410] However, such objections to Italian celebrations in the Third Ward were minute especially compared to the environment in Bay View.

While expressions of Italian culture were celebrated positively in the Third Ward by Italians and non-Italians, Bay View presented an alternative

Cultural Development Amid International Crises, 1899–1945

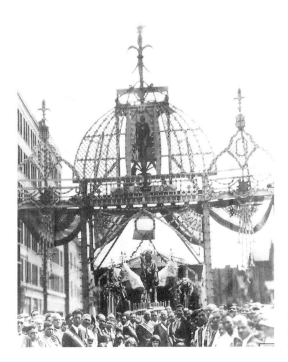

1930 St. Rocco's Italian *festa* in the Third Ward. *Photo courtesy of the Italian Community Center of Milwaukee.*

model. Immaculate Conception, Bay View's Catholic church, was led by pastor Thomas Fagan, who repeatedly referred to Italians as "dagos" and "wops" and became frustrated with the financial contributions by Bay View's Italians as well as the presence of an Italian nationalist organization, the Garibaldi Club. When members of the Garibaldi Club "insisted on wearing their tri-color nationalists sashes and buttons at funerals, Fagan was incensed at the insult" and banned them from the church.[411] Certainly not welcomed by Fagan, Bay View Italians were not welcomed to Bay View's church until the arrival of Fagan's replacement, Thomas Pierce, in 1923.[412] However, many Italians in Bay View had already decided to attend Our Lady of Pompeii in the Third Ward rather than put up with Fagan.[413] By exploring the attitudes toward Italian cultural and political expressions, one can see how the Third Ward became the cultural heart of Milwaukee's Italian community.

The Rise of an Italian-American Identity

As previously noted, the United States passed restrictive immigration quotas in 1921 and 1924. As Milwaukee's Italians gradually improved their economic positions and adopted more American customs and the educational system, particularly among second-generation immigrants, they also sought a more prominent role in American society. To do this, they continually emphasized their ties to the United States without losing their Italian identity.

The clearest example of efforts to tie Italian immigrants and their children both to the United States and to Italy was the aim by Italian leaders to push for greater recognition of Christopher Columbus. In January 1913, Assemblyman Nye introduced a measure in the Wisconsin Assembly to make October 12 "Landing Day" in honor of Columbus's landing in North America.[414] After persistence from the Italian community, Wisconsin Governor Walter Kohler signed the Columbus Day Bill on April 30, 1929, honoring the explorer.[415] In celebration of this bill, Italian societies from Kenosha, Beloit, Racine and Milwaukee all took place in a grand parade and procession in downtown Milwaukee in October 1929.[416] Far from being a minor event, over 3,500 people participated in the parade, and while seemingly a celebration of Italian pride, a photo from the *Milwaukee Sentinel* covering the parade shows several Italian-American girls holding a massive United States flag.[417] Like *feste* that were religious and cultural expressions, the Columbus Day parade emphasized the connections between the United States and Italy. The symbolism of this act was made into a tangible political objective of the Italian community in the 1930s and demonstrated not only their cultural and religious place in Milwaukee, but also their growing political and legal impact within the region.

Not satisfied with having a day noting the accomplishments of Columbus, Angelo Cerminara and hundreds of other Italians in Milwaukee pushed to make October 12 not only an annual celebration of Italian pride, but a legally recognized holiday throughout the state of Wisconsin.[418] Whereas the Italian community may not have had the political pull of other ethnic groups in Wisconsin, it waged an effective campaign to establish Columbus Day as an official holiday in 1933. By coordinating with Cerminara and Wisconsin Assembly Speaker Cornelius T. Young, Italian-American and Wisconsin Assemblyman Paul R. Alfonsi introduced legislation in January 1933 to make Columbus Day an official Wisconsin holiday.[419] Their efforts were rewarded in March 1933 as Wisconsin Governor Albert Schmedeman signed Alfonsi's measure to sign the act into law to the delight of representatives from the

Cultural Development Amid International Crises, 1899–1945

Italian communities in Wisconsin.[420] The designation of Columbus Day as an official Wisconsin holiday was an important accomplishment for the Italian community and represented a growing Italian identity within an increasingly American context.

Popular culture activities were part of a much broader trend after World War I among Italian immigrants. As Italians sent less money via remittances to their hometowns in Italy after 1910, they instead increasingly sent for family members. All of these events were part of a larger sense among Italians that "the American experience was changing from a temporary stage to a resettlement of indefinite duration."[421]

Often, aspects of American popular culture such as team sports like basketball and baseball were used to combine a sense of Americanization while at the same time emphasizing the Italian roots of the participants. For example, the Pompeii Athletic Club of Milwaukee organized an all-Italian basketball tournament at the Andrew Jackson Social Center Gym that was sponsored by local Italian businesses and had over three hundred participants in April 1934.[422] In addition to grass-roots Italian sports organizations, stories about prominent Italians in American sports such as Joe DiMaggio were commonly discussed in Milwaukee newspapers such as the *Italian Leader*.[423] Typical of other aspects of life among second-generation Italians, Italians were placed in a world that was becoming increasingly American to them.

Simultaneously, a greater Italian consciousness was emerging in Milwaukee. Milwaukee's educational leaders actively encouraged young Italians to speak the Italian language. While older residents spoke local dialects, second-generation students in the community learned to speak Italian through Milwaukee's public schools. In response, the Italian government honored Milwaukee's superintendent for increasing the education of Italian immigrants while also promoting the teaching of the Italian tongue.[424]

The 1930s witnessed a greater Italian identity through popular culture and education in Milwaukee, but also saw greater contact among Italian communities in southeastern Wisconsin. As previously mentioned, popular celebrations such as Columbus Day brought together Italians from Milwaukee, Kenosha and Racine. In the 1930s, popular culture events such as *feste* and Italian newspapers spread outside of the Milwaukee Italian community.

The *feste* that developed in the Third Ward in the late 1890s and early 1900s eventually found acceptance in Waukesha as well. In 1934, the St. Bartolomeo's *festa* thrown by Waukesha's Italians at Frame Park was very similar to those in the Third Ward and concluded with "a display of fireworks never before witnessed in Waukesha."[425] In Milwaukee's Italian community, Italian males became much more involved in church activities after the 1920s, which shifted their attitude toward the church from "casual attachment to fierce identification."[426] In December 1933, the *Italian Leader* published its first edition and, though based in Milwaukee, included whole sections devoted to the Italian communities in Madison, Waukesha and northern Wisconsin. By February 1934, 80 percent of Madison's Italians had purchased subscriptions to the *Italian Leader* and received news about their counterparts in Milwaukee and elsewhere in Wisconsin.[427] The increased attention on Italian popular culture, language and identity has caused one historian to assert that the development of an Italian identity often was often "more cogent and convincing abroad than at home."[428]

MILWAUKEE'S ITALIANS REACT TO MUSSOLINI AND WORLD WAR II

In conjunction with the shift from a regional identity to a larger American identity, there was also a renewed interest in Italy itself. This upsurge was focused on cultural affinity for Italy but was complicated by an Italian state that many had voluntarily left due to political and economic dissatisfaction. This paradox would frame the nature of Milwaukee's Italian population throughout the 1930s and World War II.

As Italians in Milwaukee established and expanded cultural celebrations in the 1920s and 1930s within a unique Italian-American context, Benito Mussolini was solidifying the transformation of Italy into a Fascist state. By 1931 Mussolini was admired by some Americans of non-Italian descent for being an innovator and as someone who "has been able to organize his people during times of peace for constructive purposes" in the midst of a chaotic Europe.[429] To Milwaukee consul Angelo Cerminara, Mussolini maximized Italian nationalism by increasing Italy's military strength while de-emphasizing regional differences, reducing crime and restoring order.[430] In 1935 the Italian State Tourist Department in Rome sponsored a contest for Italian-American students to write an article of their choosing regarding Italy.[431] The Mussolini government had a copy of the *Wisconsin News* with a story on Italian-American athletes in Milwaukee forwarded to Rome to which Cerminara was "instructed to express to you and to the fine Italian boys, the thanks and appreciation of His Excellency Mussolini."[432]

Cultural Development Amid International Crises, 1899–1945

While the relationship between Milwaukee's consulate office and Fascist Italy is difficult to ascertain, Chicago's consulate offices had increased ties with the Italian government during the Fascist years. Emigrant fraternal organizations were viewed as potential vehicles for increasing ties between emigrant communities and the Italian government. Fraternal organizations in Chicago therefore received funding from the Italian government and "became faithful purveyors of Fascist propaganda about trains running on time, the genius of Mussolini, and the inexorable rise of the 'New Italy.'"[433] The Fascist government also tried to promote its agenda by flattering Italian consuls such as Angelo Cerminara, who was given the Crown of Italy award in 1932 with the inscription, "*per grazia di dio e per volonta della nazione gran mastro della ordine della corona di Italia*," and signed by King Vittorio Emanuele III and Mussolini.[434] The Italian and non-Italian population in Wisconsin took an interest in Mussolini, which was reciprocated.

Once Italy's foreign policy became imperialistic and aggressive, support for Mussolini fluctuated. Though he admired Mussolini for consolidating Italy, Cerminara led a contingent of Italians in Milwaukee in 1933 that pushed for the United States' continued isolation from world affairs.[435] In 1935 Italy invaded Ethiopia to no great local public outcry, but Italy's support of Fascist Francisco Franco in the Spanish Civil War resulted in about twenty-five picketers outside the Italian embassy in Washington.[436] In Milwaukee, thirty-five people protested outside of the embassy calling for an end to German and Italian forces in Spain.[437] However, Cerminara also received letters from local business leaders and even Mortimer Kastner of the State Department that stated their opposition to the protesters.[438] While Milwaukeeans remained either neutral or sympathetic toward Italy in the mid-1930s, Italian communities experienced cleavages.

The 1936 Italian incursion into Ethiopia also demonstrated the extent of pan-Italianism within Milwaukee's Italian community. In 1936 Cerminara and other Italian leaders in Milwaukee donated money to the Italian Red Cross in Ethiopia. Following the Italian victory in May 1936, Italians held a victory parade in the Third Ward attended by about a thousand people. Angelo Cerminara's recommendations to the assembled crowd to "allow no feelings of inferiority to enter your minds" and to "go out into the world upon equal footing with all" were, according to a local historian, not boasts of Italian Fascist ideals, but a "quest for social honor and acceptance in America."[439] This is given further credence by the failure of the Italian-American Young Fascist Club, which was established in the city in 1933 with the goal of furthering Fascism, yet quickly petered out.[440]

When historians of Chicago's Italian-American community such as Thomas Guglielmo leave out any mention of Milwaukee, they also miss a key piece of the puzzle. The presence of a viable Italian Left in Milwaukee demonstrates the ideological conflicts that Italian Fascism posed. In 1922 the Italian Socialist Branch Society was located directly in heart of the Third Ward.[441] By the 1930s, the overwhelming majority of Milwaukee's Italians held much more moderate American political beliefs and tended to be a key Democratic constituency as witnessed by their support for Franklin Roosevelt, giving him 69 percent of their vote in 1932 and 53 percent in 1940.[442]

As the Italian government pushed Italian communities in the United States to support its war effort, there was a growing hesitancy to support Italy. Reports such as those found in *LIFE* in 1938 noted that despite Mussolini's claims of a greater Italy emerging through military and economic changes, "there is no evidence that Italy's standard of living, which is the lowest of the major powers, has been raised one jot or title since Il Duce came to power."[443] Nationally, Italian-American leaders estimated that about one-third of the 4.6 million Italian-Americans in the United States were Fascist sympathizers.[444]

Despite these criticisms by the American press, the Italian government asked Italian communities to donate jewelry for the Italian war effort. Some in the Italian community in Madison donated some items while others angrily questioned the motivations for supporting a country from which their families had emigrated largely on economic and political grounds.[445]

In New York City, anti-Fascist Carlo Tresca was assassinated in 1943, allegedly by a Mussolini supporter.[446] In Chicago, over three thousand Italian women donated their wedding rings for the war effort and in spring of 1936 were "remarried" with steel rings paid for by Mussolini in a ceremony attended by over seventy-five thousand people.[447] However, like Madison's Italian community, Chicago's Italian community was divided, and street violence even broke out between Mussolini's supporters and dissenters. In 1935 anti-Fascist leader Aldo Spero lamented to the *Chicago Tribune* that Mussolini "civilized forty million people by instituting a government by force, violence, assassination, castor-oil, and years of imprisonment imposed on everyone who disagreed with him."[448] In Milwaukee, there is no evidence of a similar drive for the Italian war effort, but one Third Ward resident whose father came to the United States in the first decade of the 1900s claimed that the community was evenly split on Mussolini.[449]

In contrast with Italians such as the Natarelli family, who were extremely discontent with the Fascist regime, other Italians in Milwaukee were sympathetic to Mussolini's Italy. One Third Ward resident resented editorials and cartoons ridiculing Mussolini and wrote that the *Milwaukee Journal* "looks more like a branch of the British foreign office than the office of an American newspaper."[450] While Italy's foreign policy decisions caused cleavages within Italian communities in the 1930s and the first two years of World War II, they would be greatly diminished once the United States entered World War II.

World War II transformed Milwaukee's Italian community and helped facilitate "Americanization" more fully while also straining family ties. After Roosevelt's "dagger in the back" speech, in which he ridiculed Italy's declaration of war against France and Great Britain in June 1940, the Italian community in Milwaukee reacted anxiously. According to the *Milwaukee Journal*, after hearing President Roosevelt's speech the atmosphere in the Third Ward was

> *not as carefree as usual. Some who can't read English called to little boys to read newspapers to them. They muttered and shook their heads sadly. The great majority attacked Mussolini and asserted that their first loyalty was to the U.S. For some, the ties of homeland are too great, and they voice cautious sentiments for Italy. Others spoke of their faith in this country but lamented some of the things President Roosevelt said about Italy and its chief. A younger fellow in another Italian rendezvous left no doubts about his feelings. "This is my homeland," he said. "I may be an Italian but I can't see what they're doing over there now. My mother was born there, but she feels the same way I do."*[451]

Once the United States entered World War II, the Italian community enthusiastically supported Roosevelt and the American war effort. In fact, 1.5 million Italian-Americans served in the United States military during World War II, which constituted over 10 percent of the United States armed services.[452] The extremely high turnout of Italian-Americans was exemplified in Milwaukee by Rose and Nunio Maniaci's family along with Domenico and Domenica Bartolone's family, both of whom had four sons in the American military.[453] According to Ann Dinsmore, "Immigrant people…always seem to have to want to prove that they're not 100 percent American [but actually] 125 percent American."[454]

When enrolling for the U.S. Navy, there was confusion over the exact date of Oswaldo Natarelli's year of birth in Abruzzo, Italy, and his uncle Sam was sent over to remedy the problem with local Italian officials. When the clerk

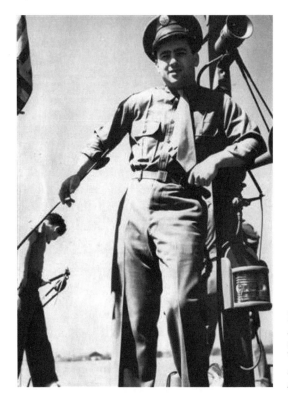

Like thousands of other Italian Americans, Mando Magnarini served in the U.S. military during World War II. *Photo courtesy of Tim Kenney, Giuseppe Garibaldi Society of Milwaukee.*

from the Italian government told Sam that Oswaldo was due for mandatory military service in Italy, Sam told the clerk that "he's in the United States Navy, you'll probably see him up here."[455]

The Italian-American role in World War II was not simply relegated to military service. As World War II became a "total war," mass production was utilized on the homefront to support the war effort. As men left for the service, manufacturing jobs, such as bottling jobs at Blatz Brewery or packaging candy for American GIs at Sperry Candy Company, were available for women.[456] As in World War I, the Italian community was asked to raise funds for American war bonds, and an effort in the Third Ward—led by Stefano Carini, Giovanni Guadalabene and Michael Dentice—yielded over $15,000.[457] Simultaneously, Stefano Carini also pursued humanitarian means to assist babies in war-torn Italy by raising money through American charities, which was sent to Italy along with three trucks of supplies.[458] Such anecdotes reveal the complexity of World War II for Milwaukee's Italians. They fully worked toward American victory yet often had relatives still living in Italy.

Therefore, the United States' conflict with Italy had a very personal impact for Milwaukee's Italians. Despite emigration from Italy being severely curtailed by the anti-immigration legislation of the 1920s, families maintained contact with relatives through the mail. However, this interaction was cut off with the outbreak of the war.[459] Therefore, there were mixed feelings in the Italian community when American and British forces invaded Sicily, where many had emigrated from.[460] Despite the public support of some Italian-Americans for Italian Fascism in the 1930s, very few Italian-Americans were interned in the United States. Unlike Japanese-Americans, those with Italian citizenship only had to register as "enemy aliens" once the United States went to war with Italy in 1941.[461]

To the relief of Italian-Americans, the invasion was short, and Italy joined the Allies shortly thereafter, removing Mussolini from power. Amazingly, a family reunion took place when Giovanni Carini was captured near Tunisia after being in the Italian navy for over six years and sent to a prisoner of war camp in Arizona. There, Giovanni was able to meet his brother, Stefano, for the first time since he was just three years old and witnessed his brother immigrate to the United States![462] This remarkable example foreshadowed the process adopted by some Italian-American families in which they would petition immigration authorities in the United States to allow Italians living abroad to be reunited with American relatives after World War II.[463] The end of World War II also marked the end of the pertinence of the Italian state to many Italian-Americans as they increasingly saw themselves as Americans, yet many maintained cultural ties to Italy.

Conclusion

Just prior to the turn of the twentieth century, Italian immigrants in Milwaukee organized unique cultural and religious celebrations known as *feste* that emulated similar celebrations in their Italian hometowns. Generally accustomed to exerting a great degree of autonomy in these festivities, Italians in Milwaukee were sometimes viewed as superstitious, rebellious and peculiar by non-Italians for their celebrations. However, when efforts to curtail these festivities failed, pressures were placed upon the immigrants to include aspects of American culture in their own unique practices. Unlike in the small towns from which many Italians emigrated, these *feste* took place in Milwaukee's urban environment and were met with both admiration and scorn by Milwaukeeans.

Despite insisting on great autonomy during parades, Italian leaders pressed for education in America's free public school system along with incorporating American displays of nationalism during and after World War I. Following World War I, anti-immigration laws were passed that curtailed the flow of migrants from Italy and coincided with an upsurge in Italian as well as American identities that differed from the regional identities that had permeated the community during the first wave of immigration. The Milwaukee community had more regular contact with other Italian "colonies" such as Madison and saw Waukesha's Italian community emulate its fireworks-centered *feste* in the 1930s. The creation of additional Italian newspapers along with the establishment of Columbus Day also fit into this influx of Italian identity in southeastern Wisconsin.

The rise of Benito Mussolini in Italy caused mixed opinions among non-Italians, while many Italians were hopeful that Mussolini would make Italy more cohesive. When Italy became imperialistic with its efforts in Ethiopia and Spain, there was some support within the community for Mussolini and the Italian war effort while others were insistent on not aiding a country that they had left due to economic and political hardships. However, "Italians abroad refused to be associated with the totalitarian regime, especially after Fascist Italy entered World War II on the side of Nazi Germany."[464] Whereas Milwaukee's Italians had sympathies with both the United States and Italy during World War I, they heavily participated in the American effort in World War II both overseas and on the homefront. Therefore, "emigrant colonialism could only be a voluntary program, and collapsed when authoritarian leaders attempted to exploit expatriate resources for aggressive war."[465]

In Milwaukee, the most successful and long-standing reminders of an Italian cultural legacy are the descendants of past popular culture displays that were embraced by the Italian and non-Italian community. In celebrations such as Festa Italiana and the wide array of Italian restaurants in the Milwaukee area, the cultural legacy of Milwaukee's Italian immigrants lives on.

Epilogue

With more restrictive immigration in the 1920s, European immigrants were replaced by African American, Mexican and Puerto Rican laborers in the United States in a process that accelerated after 1945.[466] Historian Mark Choate contends that, like Italy one hundred years earlier, migrations from emigrant countries such as India, Russia, China, Korea and Mexico in the twenty-first century can be closely studied to gain a better understanding of the impact on state policies on individuals, particularly regarding citizenship and identity.[467]

By 1945 Milwaukee's Italian-American population had spread throughout the city, with the largest concentration in the First Ward. Many took advantage of the GI Bill and moved to newly emerging suburbs while others established or expanded business endeavors that reflected their Italian ancestry. In 1955 my grandfather LeRoy "Pete" Zignego and his brother, Vernon Zignego, established Zignego Company Inc., a construction company that continues to complete major concrete projects in the Milwaukee area.[468] Long-standing Italian bastions such as the Groppi grocery store in Bay View and the relocated Busalacchi store on Brady Street joined newly emergent businesses such as Glorioso's bakery on Brady Street.[469] In comparison with the small fruit stands, grocery stores and taverns that were part of the "regional expatriate units [that] formed small economic niches and eased the uncertainties of return migration" fifty years earlier, these ethnic stores now preserved the cultural legacy of Italian Milwaukee.[470]

Epilogue

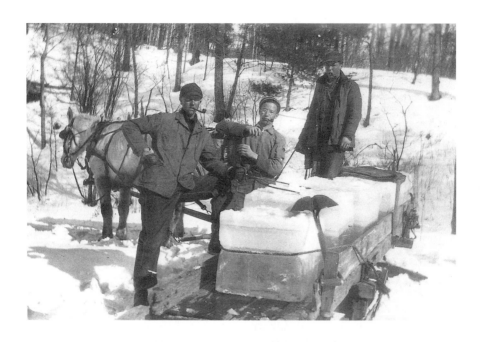

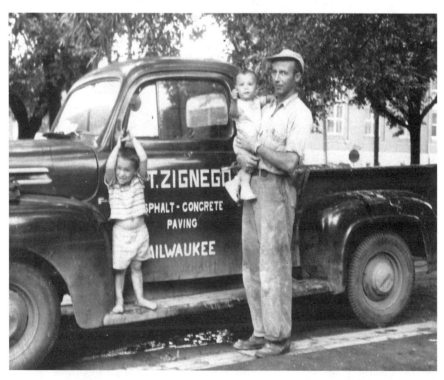

Epilogue

After being discussed since 1955, the Expressway Commission decided to purchase Our Lady of Pompeii in October 1966, and demolition began shortly thereafter.[471] T.J. Bartolotta and others in Milwaukee's community "never really got over" Pompeii's destruction.[472] Catholic priest and Marquette University history professor Steven Avella believes that Pompeii was a huge accomplishment for Milwaukee's Italian community and helped with Americanization as well as furthering an ethnic identity. However, Avella also contends that in their recollections, Italian Catholics have "wrapped a layer of romance around the small church."[473]

Along with the physical replacement of the Third Ward with a freeway and new shopping districts, there was also a sense of loss for Milwaukee's famous festivals that served important cultural functions while also entertaining and, perhaps more importantly, feeding fellow Milwaukeeans.[474] The eventual destruction of major parts of the Third Ward confirmed predictions on the neighborhood's future. In amazing clarity the *Milwaukee Sentinel* proclaimed in 1903 with reference to an 1892 fire in the neighborhood that "the Ward is rising steadily, Phoenix-like, from her ashes, and will soon be one of the busiest and prettiest wholesale districts in the country."[475]

However, Festa Italiana has served as a reunion of sorts for former Third Ward residents when it began in 1978 on the Summerfest grounds. In 1973 former residents of the Third Ward compiled a list of family and friends from the old neighborhood. By 1978 T.J. Bartolotta and others reached an agreement with Jim Butler to organize an ethnic festival on Milwaukee's lakefront with the help of over two thousand volunteers from the Italian community. Festa Italiana, as it became known, was a tremendous success, and especially famous for its nightly fireworks displays put on by Sam Bartolotta. In what T.J. Bartolotta called the "mystical magic of fireworks," Milwaukeeans could witness the colorful displays that had their roots in Milwaukee's Third Ward in the 1930s and in nineteenth-century Italy. Festa Italiana continues to this day and served as the framework to hold other ethnic festivals in Milwaukee such as Polish Fest, German Fest, Arab World Fest, Irish Fest, Mexican Fiesta and Indian Summer Festival.[476] In 1990, the Italian Community Center was built near Milwaukee's lakefront.[477]

Opposite, top: Left to right: Harvey Johnson, LeRoy "Pete" Zignego and Harry Zignego cutting ice on the Eau Galle River, near Spring Valley, Wisconsin, in 1936. *Photo courtesy of Michael Zignego.*

Opposite, bottom: The author's father, Michael, next to a Zignego Company truck, circa 1957. The author's grandfather, LeRoy "Pete" Zignego, is holding the author's uncle, Mark. *Photo courtesy of Michael Zignego.*

Epilogue

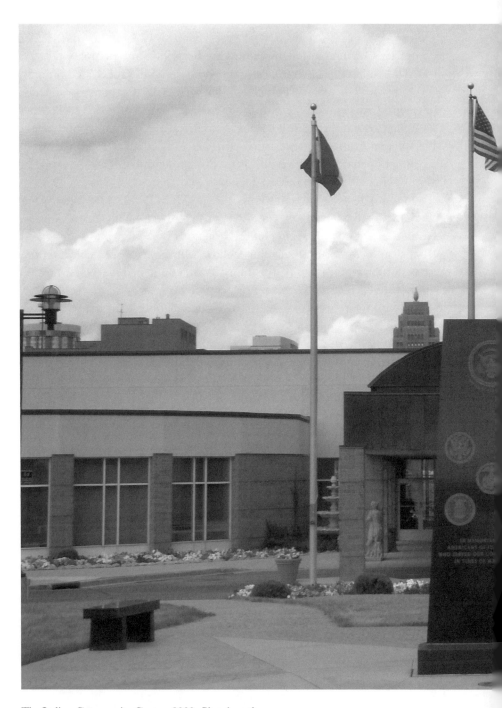

The Italian Community Center, 2009. *Photo by author.*

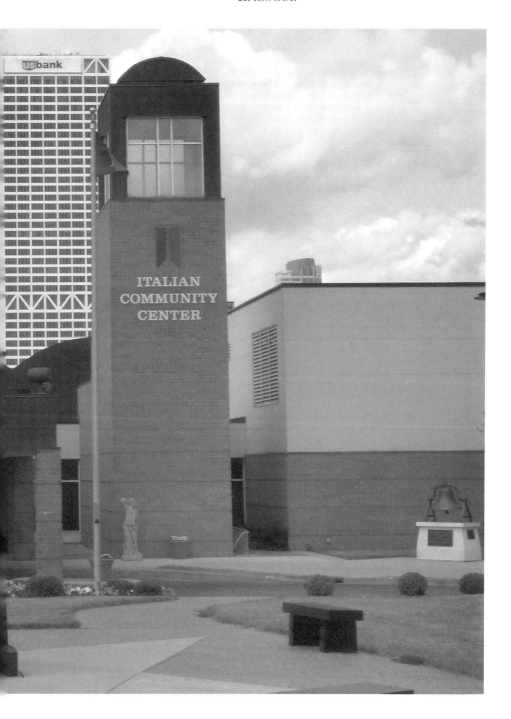

Epilogue

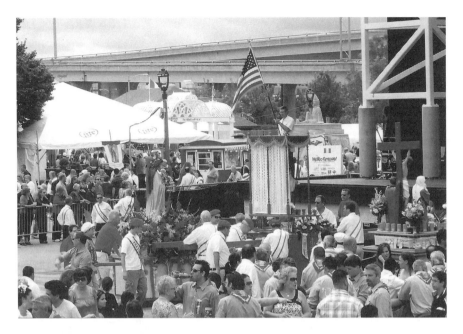

Festa Italiana, 2009. *Photo by author.*

Despite the successful revival of the celebration of Italian-American culture in Milwaukee, there are different interpretations of its impact. Milwaukee resident and author Bobby Tanzilo observed that "among Italian-Americans, I feel different because our family wasn't that stereotypical Italian-American family, since most of the stereotypes are derived from the more widespread southern Italian and Sicilian traditions."[478] Current Italian residents in 2009 have noticed the continued existence of regional tensions in Italy, yet these differences have diminished with passing generations.[479] Most Italian-Americans in the United States are now the grandchildren and great-grandchildren of Italian immigrants from multiethnic marriages, and in terms of education and occupation, "Americans of Italian descent do not differ much from other urban Americans." But, it is still very common for "Americans with hybrid roots" to "remember the 'Italian' more than other cultural origins."[480] Despite the passing of nearly eighty years between the heyday of Milwaukee's Italian-American immigrant neighborhoods, questions still remain as to what exactly it means to be an Italian-American.

Given its relatively small size, Milwaukee's Italian community has an extremely visible cultural presence compared to cities such as New York City

Epilogue

or Chicago. Milwaukee is the home of Festa Italiana, which attracts Italians from throughout the Midwest and is the most popular of Milwaukee's ethnic festivals other than Summerfest. Milwaukee also is home to the vibrant Italian Community Center, which in addition to being a successful convention center also produces a monthly newspaper, the *Italian Times*. Gardetto's has been transformed from a Bay View bakery in the 1930s into a nationally known product. The Bartolotta name synonymous with Third Ward celebrations is now recognized throughout the country as a fireworks producer. All of these amazing developments, in addition to the array of Italian restaurants, have their origins in the immigrant communities that successfully developed an Italian cultural tradition within American society.

Notes

Introduction

1. Tom Busalacchi interview, Lawrence Baldassaro collection, "Italians in Milwaukee oral history project, 1991–92," UWM Manuscript Collection 53, University of Wisconsin–Milwaukee, Box 1 Folder 6, 1–4.
2. Renee Jendusa and family, interview with author, August 2009.
3. Vecchio, *Merchants, Midwives, and Laboring Women*.
4. Carini, *Milwaukee's Italians*.
5. Gabaccia, *Italy's Many Diasporas*, 9–11.
6. Gabaccia, *From Sicily to Elizabeth Street*, 100.
7. Choate, *Emigrant Nation*.
8. Ibid., 107.
9. Carini, *Milwaukee's Italians*, 66–70.

Chapter 1

10. Choate, *Emigrant Nation*, 1.
11. Gabaccia, *Italy's Many Diasporas*, 3.
12. Choate, *Emigrant Nation*, 221–23.
13. Davis, *Short Oxford History of Italy*, 131.
14. Ibid., 74–106.

15. Ibid., 109–10.
16. Ibid., 114–18.
17. Ibid., 123–26.
18. Ibid., 127–28, 286.
19. Ibid., 123, 128.
20. Ibid., 133, 291.
21. Ibid., 139–40.
22. Ibid., 142–44.
23. Ibid., 144. My great-great-grandfather's uncle, Giovanni Zignego, was one of the Garibaldi volunteers and he sailed from Genoa with Garibaldi, near his hometown of Fezzano, to Marsala in 1860.
24. Ibid., 128–29.
25. Ibid., 144–45.
26. Ibid., 129.
27. Gabaccia, *Italy's Many Diasporas*, 50–51.
28. Davis, *Short Oxford History of Italy*, 145.
29. Ibid., 146, 286–87.
30. Ibid., 130.
31. Curtiss-Wedge, *History of Goodhue County*, 938.
32. Ibid., 147–50.
33. Zamagni, *The Economic History of Italy*, 80–84.
34. Guglielmo, *White on Arrival*, 21–22.
35. Davis, *Short Oxford History of Italy*, 145.
36. Ibid., 158–59.
37. Cinel, *National Integration of Italian Return Migration*, 32–34.
38. Ibid., 50–57.
39. Davis, *Short Oxford History of Italy*, 4–5.
40. Goldfield, *The American Journey*, 496–508.
41. Davis, *Short Oxford History of Italy*, 153.
42. Ibid., 21.
43. Choate, *Emigrant Nation*, 107.
44. Davis, *Short Oxford History of Italy*, 18.
45. Ibid., 162–63.
46. Ibid., 239–40.
47. Ibid., 183–95.
48. Ibid., 193–98.
49. Ibid., 204. In Lombardy's nine provinces, there were 3,214 parishes versus only 259 parishes in Puglia's thirty-two dioceses.

50. *Catholic Citizen*, "The Neglected Italians: Memorial to the Italian Hierarchy," September 30, 1899, 4.
51. Davis, *Short Oxford History of Italy*, 187–99.
52. Choate, *Emigrant Nation*, 7–8, 14.
53. Ibid., 24–25, 27.
54. Ibid., 28.
55. Davis, *Short Oxford History of Italy*, 168–73.
56. Choate, *Emigrant Nation*, 21.
57. Ibid., 21–29.
58. Ibid., 33–34.
59. Ibid., 35.
60. Davis, *Short Oxford History of Italy*, 178–80. Crispi's model was Otto von Bismarck's autocratic Prussia and, later, Germany.
61. Choate, *Emigrant Nation*, 37.
62. Davis, *Short Oxford History of Italy*, 180.
63. Choate, *Emigrant Nation*, 38–39.
64. Davis, *Short Oxford History of Italy*, 252–56.
65. *Catholic Citizen*, "In Catholic Circles: Father Buschart Talks on His European Trip," November 14, 1896, 5.
66. Choate, *Emigrant Nation*, 154.
67. Davis, *Short Oxford History of Italy*, 244.
68. Cinel, *National Integration of Italian Return Migration*, 23–25.
69. Davis, *Short Oxford History of Italy*, 237–38.
70. Gabaccia, *Italy's Many Diasporas*, 52.
71. Davis, *Short Oxford History of Italy*, 239.
72. Gabaccia, *Italy's Many Diasporas*, 36.
73. Ibid., 8, 53–57.
74. Choate, *Emigrant Nation*, 155.
75. Ibid., 3.
76. Salvatore Tagliavia, essay, circa 1945. Milwaukee Collection 72. University of Wisconsin–Milwaukee Archives, 3.
77. Carini, *Milwaukee's Italians*, 15–16.
78. Vecchio, *Merchants, Midwives, and Laboring Women*, 22.
79. "History of the Catalano Family," Theodore Mazza collection MSS-2290, Milwaukee County Historical Society, File 299, 7.
80. Anthony T. Machi, Baldassaro collection, Box 2 Folder 4, 1–2.
81. Meloni, "Italy Invades the Bloody Third," 48–49.
82. Gurda, *Making of Milwaukee*, 170–77.
83. Davis, *Short Oxford History of Italy*, 167, 221–24.

84. Woodall, "The Italian Massacre at Walsenburg, Colorado, 1895," 297–300.
85. Choate, *Emigrant Nation*, 15, 116–17.
86. Ibid., 48–56. Einaudi later served as the Italian president after World War II and organized postwar reconstruction.
87. Ibid., 59–61.
88. Ibid., 62.
89. Ibid., 61.
90. Ibid., 14.
91. Ibid., 23.

Chapter 2

92. Gaetanina Balistreri, Baldassaro collection, Box 1 Folder 1, 1–9.
93. Other than brief discussions of New York's Italians about remittances (Cinel, Gabaccia), this will, as far as this historian is aware, be the very first case study of Italians in a particular U.S. city that looks at return migration, immigrant remittances and relations between Italian expatriates and the Italian government in this period.
94. Andreozzi, "Contadini and Pescatori," 29–36.
95. *Catholic Citizen*, "New Priest at Italian Mission," July 18, 1903.
96. Ibid., 3.
97. Avella, *In the Richness of the Earth*, 242–43.
98. Gabaccia, *Italy's Many Diasporas*, 5–6, 72.
99. Cinel, *National Integration of Italian Return Migration*, 8.
100. Ibid., 98–99.
101. Gabaccia, *Italy's Many Diasporas*, 80.
102. Choate, *Emigrant Nation*, 8–9.
103. Crawford, "About Italian Immigration," reprint appeared in the September 20, 1907 edition of the *Catholic Citizen*, 4.
104. Ibid.
105. Angelo Cerminara collection, "Italians of Milwaukee in This Country to Stay: Life is New for Them," news clipping, MSS-0216, Milwaukee County Historical Society, Folder 11.
106. Gaetanina Balisteri, Baldassaro collection, Box 1 Folder 1, 2–10. Gaetano subsequentially had the eye surgery, returned to the United States in 1911 and established his own saloon at 571 Canal Street.
107. *Catholic Citizen*, "The Italian Hegira," December 1, 1906, 3.

108. Choate, *Emigrant Nation*, 156.
109. Ibid., 72–73.
110. Cinel, *National Integration of Italian Return Migration*, 107–11.
111. Rudy Bertolas, Baldassaro collection, Box 1 Folder 4, 1–4.
112. Choate, *Emigrant Nation*, 80.
113. Cinel, *National Integration of Italian Return Migration*, 129–31. *Padrone* has many different meanings in Italian but was usually used to describe respected leaders in the community.
114. Ibid., 131.
115. Ibid., 126–31.
116. Ibid., 132–139.
117. Ibid., 136–40.
118. Ibid., 133–34.
119. *Catholic Citizen*, January 11, 1908, 3.
120. Tagliavia, "The Development of the Milwaukee Settlements," 2.
121. Columbia Savings Bank advertisement, "Columbiana: A Historical Souvenir of the Columbian Celebration." Held under the Auspices of the Italian Societies of the State of Wisconsin in Milwaukee, WI, October 1929, Cerminara collection, MCHS, Folder 12, p. 49 in booklet.
122. Ibid.
123. Pizzino and Montag, *Peter's Story*, 80.
124. "Il Banco di Napoli," official charter certificate to Angelo Cerminara from the general director of the Banco di Napoli (Bank of Naples), April 25, 1918, Cerminara collection, MCHS, Folder 2.
125. Choate, *Emigrant Nation*, 155.
126. Ibid., 156–57.
127. *Catholic Citizen*, "Rebirth of Italy: Wonderful Growth of the Italians in Material Prosperity. Latins Coming to the Front. Becoming a Great Manufacturing Nation," December 1, 1906, 3.
128. Choate, *Emigrant Nation*, 189–90, 200–01.
129. *Free Press*, "Sad Case is Told," December 30, 1908, Cerminara collection, MCHS, Folder 11.
130. Choate, *Emigrant Nation*, 202–03.
131. Ibid., 94–96.
132. Ibid., 16–71.
133. Ibid., 174–76.
134. *Free Press*, "Italians Celebrate the Establishment of Peace: Speaker Says Mother Country Could not Have Won Without American Sons' Help," November 12, 1912, Cerminara collection, MCHS.

135. Ibid.
136. Choate, *Emigrant Nation*, 179.
137. *Free Press*, "Italians Celebrate," Cerminara collection, MCHS.
138. Choate, *Emigrant Nation*, 204.
139. *Free Press*, "Institute New Plan to Aid Countrymen: Italian Government Will Exercise Fatherly Care Over People," August 1911, Cerminara collection, MCHS, Folder 11.
140. Choate, *Emigrant Nation*, 208–15.
141. *Evening Wisconsin*, "Milwaukee Men Who Are Making History in Drafting the Aliens," September 26, 1917, Cerminara collection, MCHS, Folder 11.
142. Ibid.
143. "Italian Exodus Predicted," March 2, Cerminara collection, MCHS, loose news clipping, Folder 11.
144. Angelo Cerminara, "Historic Precedent," *Evening Wisconsin*, January 22, Cerminara collection, MCHS, news clipping, Folder 11.
145. Robert Tanzilo papers, "Garibaldi Society Minutes," Immigration History Research Center, University of Minnesota, Box 1 Envelope 3 Log # 1011, 14.
146. Choate, *Emigrant Nation*, 203.
147. Erich C. Stern, "Erich Cramer Stern Papers: 1868–1967," Milwaukee Mss EM, University of Wisconsin–Milwaukee Archives, Folders 12 and 16.
148. *Evening Wisconsin*, "Ad un Professore di Sociologia," February 19, 1914, Cerminara collection, MCHS, Folder 11.
149. Guglielmo, *White on Arrival*, 23.
150. La Piana, *The Italians in Milwaukee, WI*, 7.
151. *Evening Wisconsin*, "Ad un Professore di Sociologia," Cerminara collection, MCHS MCHS.
152. Choate, *Emigrant Nation*, 214, 296. Quoted from Wilson's *History of the American People* (New York: 1902), 4: 212–14, 300. Likewise, Wilson also praised what he perceived to be the positive virtues of Jim Crow legislation in the southern United States, adding that southern "sections began to draw together with a new understanding of one another."
153. Guglielmo, *White on Arrival*, 23–24.
154. Ibid., 23.
155. Avella, *In the Richness of the Earth*, 208.
156. Wolfensberger, "Woodrow Wilson," 11–12.
157. Choate, *Emigrant Nation*, 216–17.

Chapter 3

158. Addams, *Twenty Years at Hull-House*, 232.
159. Guglielmo, *White on Arrival*, 60.
160. Ibid., 38–56.
161. Gabaccia, *From Sicily to Elizabeth Street*, 8–13.
162. Ibid., 18–22.
163. Ibid., 52.
164. Vincent Emanuele, Baldassaro collection, Box 1 Folder 10, 4–5.
165. Gurda, "The Church and the Neighborhood," 6.
166. Gurda, *The Making of Milwaukee*, 176.
167. Meloni, "Italy Invades the Bloody Third," 48.
168. Tony Dicristo, Baldassaro collection, Box 1 Folder 9, 11.
169. LeRoy Bertocini, Baldassaro collection, Box 1 Folder 5, 22.
170. Choate, *Emigrant Nation*, 106.
171. Carini, *Milwaukee's Italians*, 24. Ref. to 1910 U.S. census report.
172. Choate, *Emigrant Nation*, 156.
173. Carini, *Milwaukee's Italians*, 99.
174. Ibid., 28–29, 34.
175. Meloni, "Italy Invades the Bloody Third," 47.
176. Gaetanina Balistreri, Baldassaro collection, Box 1 Folder 5, 7.
177. LeRoy Bertocini, Baldassaro collection, Box 1 Folder 5, 7.
178. Meloni, "Italy Invades the Bloody Third," 49.
179. *Milwaukee Journal*, "All Milwaukee Italians Aren't in Third Ward," December 5, 1926, 10.
180. La Piana, *The Italians in Milwaukee, WI*, 8.
181. Avella, *In the Richness of the Earth*, 248. Groppi's grocery store was located on the corner of Russell and Wentworth in 1912.
182. Robert Tanzilo papers, "Little Italy: Lifelong friendships began in Bay View neighborhood," Immigration History Research Center, University of Minnesota, Box 1 LOG #1005.
183. Meloni, "Italy Invades the Blood Third," 49–51.
184. Simonsen, "The Third Ward," 62, referring to 1906 Department of Labor Report.
185. Vecchio, *Merchants, Midwives, and Laboring Women*, 62.
186. Meloni, "Italy Invades the Bloody Third," 51, referring to *A World Movement and Its American Significance* by Henry Fairchild, 1926. (For an account of a Milwaukee visitor to 1896 Naples, please see Chapter 2, 16.)
187. La Piana, *The Italians in Milwaukee, WI*, 14–15.

188. Simonsen, "The Third Ward," 62.
189. La Piana, *The Italians in Milwaukee, WI*, 15.
190. Pizzino and Montag, *Peter's Story*, 18.
191. Gabaccia, *Elizabeth Street*, 71–74. The rent was the average paid for an Elizabeth Street apartment in New York between 1900 and 1910, and represented about one third of an Italian laborer's monthly income of $475 per year.
192. Tagliavia, "The Development of the Milwaukee Settlements," 10.
193. Carini, *Milwaukee's Italians*, 29.
194. Ibid., 43.
195. Gabaccia, *Elizabeth Street*, 93.
196. Ibid., 107–08.
197. Carini, *Milwaukee's Italians*, 28.
198. Simonsen, "The Third Ward," 66.
199. Cinel, *National Integration of Italian Return Migration*, 157–08.
200. Tom Busalacchi, Baldassaro collection, Box 1 Folder 6, 1–6.
201. Carini, *Milwaukee's Italians*, Appendix XIII, A. 16.
202. Tom Busalacchi, Baldassaro collection, 6–10.
203. Ibid., 5–11.
204. Oswald Natarelli, Baldassaro collection, Box 2 Folder 5, 1–5.
205. Ann Romano, "Wisconsin Women during World War II Oral History Project Interviews, 1992–94," Mss 844; Tape 1255A; PH Mss 844A & B, Wisconsin Historical Society Archives, Box 6 Folder 2.
206. "Resconto Finanziario Della Chiesa," Madonna Di Pompompei Per'L Anno 1934, Milwaukee Archdiocese Archives, Blessed Virgin of Pompeii Folder AS: 1, booklet.
207. Ibid. The only non-Italian surname was Annuziata Laskowski, presumably of Polish-Italian origins.
208. Tagliavia, "The Development of the Milwaukee Settlements," 18–20.
209. Gurda, "The Church and Neighborhood," 17.
210. Tagliavia, "The Development of the Milwaukee Settlements," 8. The 1930 U.S. Census notes 4,986 Italians overall living among Milwaukee's 578,249 residents.
211. Antoinette Carini, Baldassaro collection, Box 1 Folder 7, 10–11.
212. Owald Natarelli, Baldassaro collection, Box 2 Folder 5, 9–10.
213. Pizzino and Montag, *Peter's Story*, 38.
214. Carini, *Milwaukee's Italians*, 62.
215. Vincent Emanuele, Baldassaro collection, Folder 10, 7.
216. Oswald Natarelli, Baldassaro collection, Box 2 Folder 5, 9.

217. Vincent Emanuele, Baldassaro collection, Box 1 Folder 10, 4.
218. Ibid., 4–5.
219. Ibid., 5.
220. Pizzino and Montag, *Peter's Story*, 7, 33–34, 84.
221. Grace Falbo, Baldassaro collection, Box 1 Folder 12, 7–8.
222. Rudy Bertolas, Baldassaro collection, Box 1 Folder 4, 3–5.
223. Ibid., 7–9.
224. Gabaccia, *Elizabeth Street*, 109.
225. Cinel, *National Integration of Italian Return Migration*, 55–56, 194.
226. Carini, *Milwaukee's Italians*, 61.
227. Ibid., 18–19.
228. Vecchio, *Merchants, Midwives, and Laboring Women*, 78.
229. Meloni, "Italy Invades the Bloody Third," 51.
230. Vecchio, *Merchants, Midwives, and Laboring Women*, 66–68.
231. Pizzino and Montag, *Peter's Story*, 67–68.
232. LeRoy Bertocini, Baldassaro collection, Box 1 Folder 5, 7.
233. Ibid., 3.
234. Pizzino and Montag, *Peter's Story*, 72–73.
235. Elsie M. Falbo, Baldassaro collection, Box 1 Folder 11, 4–7, 16.
236. Grace Falbo, Baldassaro collection, Box 1 Folder 12, 4–6.
237. Tony Seidita, Baldassaro collection, Box 2 Folder 8, 6. The 1922 Milwaukee City Directory lists Jack and Mamie Sibrigandio as the owners of "J. Seidita & Co." and their residence as 165 Huron Street (p. 1485).
238. Ibid., 8.
239. Ibid., 8–9.
240. Pizzino and Montag, *Peter's Story*, 57–60.
241. "Jewish Youth to hear Italian Consul," news clipping, Cerminara collection, MCHS, Folder 8.
242. "Opening Celebration of The Beulah Brinton Community House," October 13–17, 1924, Conducted by Milwaukee Board of School Directors Extension Department, Cerminara collection, Loose program, Folder 8, 3.
243. Frank Gross Jr., "Letter to Rev. E.T. Sandoval," May 24, 1926, Milwaukee Archdiocese Archives, Frank Gross Jr. Papers MC 158, Box 1 Folder 3, loose item.
244. Provi Jendusa, interview with author, August 2009.
245. Robert Tanzilo Papers, Immigration History Research Center, University of Minnesota, "Little Italy: Lifelong friendships began in Bay View neighborhood," Box 1 LOG # 1005.

246. Carini, *Milwaukee's Italians*, 66–70.
247. Greene, "Dealing With Diversity," 828–32.
248. *Italian Leader* 1, no. 7, "Milwaukee News: The Italian Section Tour," June 1934, 8.
249. Vincent Emanuele, Baldassaro collection, Box 1 Folder 10, 12.
250. Ibid., 12–14.
251. Grace Falbo, Baldassaro collection, Box 1 Folder 12, 20.
252. Gabaccia, *Elizabeth Street*, 81–82.
253. T.J. Bartolotta, "I Remember Milwaukee: T.J. Bartolotta, Program 134," 1995, University of Wisconsin–Milwaukee Library, VHS-2751.
254. Simonsen, "The Third Ward," 61.

Chapter 4

255. Josephine Rampolla, Baldassaro collection, Box 2 Folder 7, 2.
256. Ibid., 4–7.
257. Vecchio, *Merchants, Midwives, and Laboring Women*, 2.
258. Ibid., Chapter 3 "Gender, Economic Opportunities, and Italian Businesswomen in Milwaukee," 61–83.
259. Gabaccia, *Elizabeth Street*, 4–6.
260. Ibid., 44.
261. Ibid., 46.
262. Gabaccia, *Italy's Many Diasporas*, 88.
263. Noether, "The Silent Half," 6.
264. Gabaccia, *Elizabeth Street*, 46.
265. Gabaccia, *From the Other Side*, 101.
266. Noether, "The Silent Half," 4.
267. Gabaccia, *From the Other Side*, 102.
268. Noether, "The Silent Half," 5.
269. Gabaccia, *From the Other Side*, 30.
270. Ibid., 37–38.
271. Vecchio, *Merchants, Midwives, and Laboring Women*, 14–16.
272. Ibid., 4–6, 18–20, 32–60.
273. Ibid., 3–4.
274. Ibid., 23–29.
275. Cinel, *National Integration of Italian Return Migration*, 103–06.
276. Gabaccia, *Italy's Many Diasporas*, 74.
277. Ibid., 74–77.

278. Lawrence Jendusa, interview with author, February 2009.
279. Gabaccia, *Italy's Many Diasporas*, 77–78.
280. La Piana, *The Italians in Milwaukee, WI*, 10–12.
281. LeRoy Bertocini, Baldassaro collection, Box 1 Folder 5, 8–9.
282. Tagliavia, "The Development of the Milwaukee Settlements," 9–10.
283. Vecchio, *Merchants, Midwives, and Laboring Women*, 64–65.
284. Ibid.
285. Antoinette Carini, Baldassaro collection, Box 1 Folder 7, 2–3.
286. Vecchio, *Merchants, Midwives, and Laboring Women*, 69–70, 74.
287. Ibid., 70.
288. Antoinette Carini, Baldassaro collection, Box 1 Folder 7, 8.
289. Vecchio, *Merchants, Midwives, and Laboring Women*, 70.
290. Gaetanina Balisteri, Baldassaro collection, Box 1 Folder 1, 1.
291. Ibid., Box 1 Folder 1, 17.
292. Antoinette Carini, Baldassaro collection, Box 1 Folder 7, 8.
293. Tagliavia, "The Development of the Milwaukee Settlements," 9.
294. Vecchio, *Merchants, Midwives, and Laboring Women*, 71–74.
295. Ibid., 76.
296. Gabaccia, *From the Other Side*, 46.
297. Antoinette Carini, Baldassaro collection, Box 1 Folder 7, 4.
298. Anthony Dicristo, Balassaro collection, Box 1 Folder 9, 1–10.
299. Josephine Rampolla, Baldassaro collection, Box 2 Folder 7, 8.
300. Gaetanina Balisteri, Baldassaro collection, Box 1 Folder 1, 17–19. Her father was working as a crane operator in the Third Ward in 1924.
301. Grace M. Falbo, Baldassaro collection, Box 1 Folder 12, 1–2.
302. *Italian Leader* 1, no. 3, "Ladies Page," February 1934, 9.
303. Gabaccia, *Elizabeth Street*, 46–47.
304. Josephine Rampolla, Baldassaro collection, Box 2 Folder 7, 12.
305. Jennie Firmano, "Wisconsin Women during World War," Box 3 Folder 1, 7.
306. Anthony T. Machi, Baldassaro collection, Box 2 Folder 4, 16.
307. Mary Ann Sarsfield Koerner, Baldassaro collection, Box 2 Folder 3, 9–10.
308. Josephine Rampolla, Baldassaro collection, Box 2 Folder 7, 6.
309. Vecchio, *Merchants, Midwives, and Laboring Women*, 79–83.
310. Mary Ann Sarsfield Koerner, Baldassaro collection, Box 2 Folder 3, 6.
311. Carini, *Milwaukee's Italians*, 32–33.
312. Anthony Discristo, Baldassaro collection, Box 1 Folder 9, 4–8.
313. Gabaccia, *From the Other Side*, 48–50.

314. Tom Busalacchi, Baldassaro collection, Box 1 Folder 6, 8–9.
315. Mary Sorgi, "Wisconsin Women during World War II," Box 6 Folder 14, 1–6.
316. Antoinette Carini, Baldassaro collection, Box 1 Folder 7, 10.
317. 1930 City of Milwaukee Directory, 304.
318. Antoinette Carini, Baldassaro collection, Box 1 Folder 7, 11.
319. Gabaccia, *From the Other Side*, 51–52.
320. 1930 City of Milwaukee Directory, 1406.
321. Andreozzi, "Contadini and Pescatori," 35.
322. Gabaccia, *Elizabeth Street*, 80.
323. Carini, *Milwaukee's Italians*, 52.
324. LeRoy Bertocini, Baldassaro collection, Box 1 Folder 5, 6.
325. Meloni, "Italy Invades the Bloody Third," 53.
326. LeRoy Bertocini, Baldassaro collection, Box 1 Folder 5, 6.
327. Carini, *Milwaukee's Italians*, 52–53.
328. Tagliavia, "The Development of the Milwaukee Settlements," 4.
329. Gabaccia, *Elizabeth Street*, 9.
330. Gurda, "Church and Neighborhood," 5.
331. Carini, *Milwaukee's Italians*, 103–04.
332. Andreozzi, "Contadini and Pescatori," 123.
333. Carini, *Milwaukee's Italians*, 102–03.
334. "Little Pink Church" (Pompeii), Milwaukee Public Library, Viewed at UW–Milwaukee Library December 2008, VHS 0589.
335. Gurda, "Church and Community," 15.
336. Carini, *Milwaukee's Italians*, 76–79.
337. Gabaccia, *From the Other Side*, 84.
338. "Articles of Incorporation of Casa Italiana," Cerminara collection, Milwaukee County Historical Society, Folder 1, 1–3. Emphasis added.
339. Angelo Cerminara, letter to Miss Anita Sorgi, July 27, 1933, Cerminara collection, Folder 1.
340. Gabaccia, *From the Other Side*, 84.
341. Gaetanina Balistreri, Baldassarro collection, Box 1 Folder 1, 2–5.
342. Tagliavia, "The Development of the Milwaukee Settlements," 4.
343. Gaetanina Balistreri, Baldassarro collection, Box 1 Folder 1, 9, 13–14.
344. Gabaccia, *Italy's Many Diasporas*, 98.
345. Cinel, *National Integration of Italian Return Migration*, 123.
346. Pizzino and Montag, *Peter's Story*, 102. As far as I know, he is not related to the New York Yankees baseball player.
347. City of Milwaukee Directory 1930, 503.

348. Pizzino and Montag, *Peter's Story*, 175.
349. Anthony Dicristo, Baldassaro collection, Box 1 Folder 9, 12–22.
350. Pizzino and Montag, *Peter's Story*, 34–35, 38.
351. Gaetanina Balistreri, Baldassaro collection, Box 1 Folder 1, 12–13.
352. Antoinette Carini, Baldassaro collection, Box 1 Folder 7, 14.
353. Anthony Dicristo, Baldassaro collection, Box 1 Folder 9, 18–19.
354. Ann Romano, "Wisconsin Women during World War II," Box 6 Folder 2, 7.
355. Anthony T. Machi, Baldassaro collection, Box 2 Folder 4, 16.
356. Grace Falbo, Baldassaro collection, Box 1 Folder 12, 25.
357. Pizzino and Montag, *Peter's Story*, 8–9.
358. Ibid., 47.
359. Gabaccia, *Italy's Many Diasporas*, 7.
360. Cinel, *National Integration of Italian Return Migration*, 96.
361. Jennie Firmano, "Wisconsin Women during World War II," Box 3, Folder 1, 1.
362. Thomas Hemman, "In Memoriam," *Italian Times*, January 2009, Vol. 30, No. 7, 14.

Chapter 5

363. Oswald Natarelli, Baldassaro collection, Box 2 Folder 5, 1–2, 17–18.
364. Ibid., Box 2 Folder 5, 16.
365. Phillip Firmano, Baldassaro collection, Box 2 Folder 1, 3–7.
366. LeRoy Bertocini, Baldassarro collection, Box 1 Folder 5, 6.
367. Tony Seidita, Baldassarro collection, Box 2 Folder 8, 22.
368. Mary Ann Koerner Sarsfield, Baldassarro collection, Box 2 Folder 3, 15.
369. Antoinette Carini, Baldassarro collection, Box 1 Folder 7, 15.
370. *Catholic Citizen*, "Italians Celebrate: Feast of St. Joseph Celebrated in Their Own Unique Manner by the Italian Colony," March 25, 1899, 5.
371. *Catholic Citizen*, "The Neglected Italians: Memorial to the Italian Hierarchy," September 30, 1899, 4.
372. Avella, *In the Richness of the Earth*, 241.
373. Gurda, "Church and Neighborhood," 13.
374. *Catholic Citizen*, "Fr. Rosario's Italian Mission," September 30, 1899, 5.
375. Avella, *In the Richness of the Earth*, 242.

376. Gurda, "Church and Neighborhood," 14.
377. Carini, *Milwaukee's Italians*, 98–100.
378. Gurda, "Church and Neighborhood," 15.
379. Davis, *Short Oxford History of Italy*, 183–85.
380. Carini, *Milwaukee's Italians*, 80–82.
381. *Catholic Citizen*, "Disapproves Italian Celebrations," December 1, 1906.
382. Gabaccia, *Elizabeth Street*, 50.
383. *Catholic Citizen*, "Disapproves Italian Celebrations," December 1, 1906.
384. Avella, *In the Richness of the Earth*, 495.
385. Choate, *Emigrant Nation*, 132–46.
386. LeRoy Bertocini, Baldassarro collection, Box 1 Folder 5, 18.
387. Gurda, *The Making of Milwaukee*, 176–77.
388. Tony Seidita, Baldassarro collection, Box 2 Folder 8, 19.
389. *Catholic Citizen*, "Italians Have Gala Celebration," September 26, 1908, 3.
390. *Catholic Citizen*, "In Catholic Circles," February 9, 1907, 3.
391. "Italians Dedicate Beautiful Flags: Distinguished Guests Present in Father Matthew Hall and Banquet at Dania Hall," Angelo Cerminara collection, MCHS, Folder 11. This is a news clipping from an undated paper, though Racine Mayor A. J. Horlick served from 1907 to 1911.
392. Ibid.
393. Ibid.
394. Carini, *Milwaukee's Italians*, 67–69.
395. Greene, "Dealing with Diversity," 830.
396. Robert Tanzilo, "Politics, Protest and Proselytization: A Struggle Among Italian-Americans in 1917 Milwaukee" (unpublished book, 2007).
397. "Sane Fourth Independence Day Milwaukee-1918," Angelo Cerminara collection, MCHS, Folder 10.
398. Mary Ann Sarsfield Koerner, Baldassarro collection, Box 2 Folder 3, 16.
399. Greene, "Dealing with Diversity," 827.
400. Ibid., 828–32.
401. Ibid., 838.
402. Ibid., 838–44.
403. "Remember When…" news clipping, Angelo Cerminara collection, MCHS.

404. Sam Purpero, Baldassarro collection, Box 2 Folder 6, 26.
405. Pizzino and Montag, *Peter's Story*, 48.
406. Charlotte Gower, "The Feast of San Giuseppe," *Italian Leader* 1, no. 4, March 1934, 3, 11.
407. *Italian Leader* 1, no. 8, "La Festa San Giuseppe," July 1934, 7.
408. T.J. Bartolotta Interview.
409. Greene, "Dealing with Diversity," 832–33. Referring to *The Milwaukee Journal*, March 26, 27, 30 and April 2–4, 1928.
410. Avella, *In the Richness of the Earth*, 495.
411. Ibid., 248.
412. Anna Passante, "Remembering Bay View's Little Italy," *Bay View Compass: The South Shore Bellwether*, July 2007, vol. 4 no. 7, 5.
413. Avella, *In the Richness of the Earth*, 248–49.
414. "State of Wisconsin: In Assembly," No. 113, A, January 26, 1913, Cerminara collection, MCHS, Box 1 Folder 4.
415. Carini, *Milwaukee's Italians*, 84.
416. *Chicago Daily Tribune*, "Columbus Day Celebration Brings Thousands of Visitors to Milwaukee," Cerminara collection, MCHS, Box 1 Folder 8.
417. *Milwaukee Sentinel*, "Thousands 'In Step' as Colorful Observance of Columbus Day," October 14, 1929, Cerminara collection, MCHS, Box 1 Folder 8.
418. *Milwaukee Sentinel*, "Italians See Columbus Day as Legal Holiday in State," October 13, 1931, Cerminara collection, MCHS, Box 1 Folder 4.
419. Cornelius T. Younger, letter to Angelo Cerminara, January 24, 1933, Cerminara collection, MCHS, Box 1 Folder 4.
420. *Wisconsin State Journal*, "Governor Signs 'Landing Day' Bill," March 26, 1933, Cerminara collection, MCHS, Box 1 Folder 4.
421. Cinel, *National Integration of Italian Return Migration*, 140–41.
422. *Italian Leader* 1, no. 6, "The Third Ward Tournament," May 1934, 16.
423. Sal Foti, "Italians Raid Baseball in Droves," *Italian Leader* 3, no. 4, March 1, 1936, 4.
424. Carini, *Milwaukee's Italians*, 65–70.
425. *Italian Leader* 1, no. 10, "Wisconsin's Italians: Waukesha," September 1934, 8.
426. Gurda, "From Church to Neighborhood," 15.
427. *Italian Leader* 1, no. 3, "Gratitude," February 1934, 2.

428. Choate, *Emigrant Nation*, 105.
429. *Fond Du Lac Commonwealth Reporter*, "Italy Training Its Youth as Security for Future Days; Consul in Rotary Address," April 21, 1931, Cerminara collection, MCHS, Folder 8.
430. Cerminara collection, MCHS, Folder 8.
431. *Italian Leader* 2, no. 10, "A Contest for Best Article on Italy," May 5, 1935, 2.
432. *Wisconsin News*, Stefano Carini collection, MCHS, Folder 96, loose clipping.
433. Guglielmo, *White on Arrival*, 113–16.
434. Crown of Italy Award 1932, April 18, 1932, Cerminara collection, Folder 5. The English translation reads "for grace of God and will of the nation great master of the order of the crown of Italy."
435. *Wisconsin News*, "Italians Here Declare for National Isolation," news clipping, February 1933, Stefano Carini collection, MCHS, Box 3 Folder 95.
436. *Italian Leader* 5, no. 14, "Picketing the Italian Embassy," April 9, 1937.
437. *Wisconsin News*, news clipping, June 5, 1937, Cerminara collection, MCHS, Folder 6.
438. Mortimer Kastner and Matt H. Carpenter, Letters to Angelo Cerminara, June 5, 1937, Cerminara collection, MCHS, Folder 6.
439. Andreozzi, "Contadini and Pescatori," 84–85. Cerminara quoted from the *Milwaukee Journal*, May 11, 1936, sec. 1, 11.
440. Ibid., 84.
441. 1922 City of Milwaukee Directory, 807. The Socialist Branch Society was located at 189 Detroit Street. Amazingly, Guglielmo's *White on Arrival* does not contain a single reference to Milwaukee in its 294 pages.
442. Carini, *Milwaukee's Italians*, 86
443. *LIFE*, "Fascism: Inside Italy There is Also 'The Corporative State,'" May 9, 1938, 31.
444. Gabaccia, *Italy's Many Diasporas*, 146–47.
445. Ann Romano, "Wisconsin Women during World War II," Box 6 Folder 2, 2–3. Certainly, a sensitive topic for Italian-Americans, there is no evidence of similar fundraising efforts made in Milwaukee.
446. Gabaccia, *Italy's Many Diasporas*, 148–49.
447. Guglielmo, *White on Arrival*, 118–19.
448. Ibid., 116.
449. Tony Dicristo, Baldassaro collection, Box 1 Folder 9, 23.

450. John L. Vicini, "From the People: Heil Il Duce!," *Milwaukee Journal*, June 18, 1941.
451. Andreozzi, "Contadini and Pescatori," 86–88. Quoted from the *Milwaukee Journal*, June 11, 1940 (late edition), 1.
452. "Italian-American Contributions," accessed February 25, 2009.
453. Carini, *Milwaukee's Italians*, 60.
454. Ann Dinsmore, "Wisconsin Women during World War II," Box 2 Folder 10, 2–3.
455. Oswald Natarelli, Baldassaro collection, Box 2 Folder 5, 16–18.
456. Ann Romano, "Wisconsin Women during World War II," Box 6 Folder 2, 1–4.
457. Stefano Carini Obituary, Stefano Carini collection, MCHS, Folder 7.
458. Secretary of the Columbus Center, "To Whom it May Concern," Stefano Carini collection, MCHS, Folder 7.
459. Ann Romano, "Wisconsin Women during World War II," Box 6 Folder 2, 3.
460. Mary Sorgi, "Wisconsin Women during World War II," Box 6 Folder 2, 10.
461. Gabaccia, *Italy's Many Diasporas*, 148–49.
462. Loise Cattoi, "One Stayed in Sicily; One Came to America; Brothers Long Parted Meet in Prison Camp," *Milwaukee Journal*, news clipping, September 14, 1943, Stefano Carini collection, Folder 8.
463. Stefano Carini, Letter to U.S. Immigration Authority, September 29, 1948, Stefano Carini collection, MCHS, Folder 98.
464. Choate, *Emigrant Nation*, 231.
465. Ibid.

Epilogue

466. Gabaccia, *Italy's Many Diasporas*, 135–36.
467. Choate, *Emigrant Nation*, 218–33.
468. 1955 Milwaukee City Directory.
469. 27th Annual Columbus Day Banquet Program, October 14, 1956, Cerminara collection, MCHS, Folder 10.
470. Choate, *Emigrant Nation*, 107.
471. Simonsen, "The Third Ward," 67–70.
472. T.J. Bartolotta, "I Remember Milwaukee: T.J. Bartolotta, Program 134."

473. Avella, *In the Richness of the Earth*, 250–51.
474. Charlie House, "Italians Arrived Late, but Total Swelled," *Milwaukee Journal*, November 18, 1966, 6.
475. *Milwaukee Sentinel*, January 5, 1903. Reference contained within Meloni's article, 59.
476. T.J. Bartolotta, "I Remember Milwaukee: T.J. Bartolotta, Program 134."
477. Gurda, *Making of Milwaukee*, 403–04.
478. Robert Tanzilo Papers, Immigration History Research Center, University of Minnesota, "Piedmontesi-Americans: An Oral History Project," Box 1 Envelope 1.
479. Michele Zignego, interview with author, January 2009.
480. Gabaccia, *Italy's Many Diasporas*, 183–84.

Bibliography

Primary Sources

Addams, Jane. *Twenty Years at Hull-House with Autobiographical Notes*. New York: Macmillan, 1910.

Baldassaro, Lawrence. "Italians in Milwaukee oral history project, 1991–1992." UWM Manuscript Collection 53. University of Wisconsin–Milwaukee.

Bartolotta, T.J. *I Remember Milwaukee*. T.J. Bartolotta, Program 134. VHS-2751. Milwaukee: University of Wisconsin-Milwaukee Library, 1995.

Carini, Stefano. Papers. Milwaukee County Historical Society, Milwaukee.

Catholic Citizen, 1896–1908.

Cerminara, Angelo. Angelo Cerminara Collection. Milwaukee County Historical Society, Milwaukee, WI.

Gross, Frank Jr. Papers. Milwaukee Archdiocese Archives, Milwaukee, May 24, 1926. Folder 3.

Italian Leader, December 1933–April 1937.

Jendusa, Lawrence. Interview with author, February 2009.

Jendusa, Provi. Interview with author, August 2009.

Jendusa, Renee. Interview with author, August 2009.

La Piana, George. 1915. *The Italians in Milwaukee, WI: General Survey*. Reprint, San Francisco: R&E Research Associates, 1970.

Life, "Fascism: Inside Italy There is Also 'The Corporative State,'" May 9, 1938.

Little Pink Church (Pompeii). Milwaukee Public Library, viewed at UW-Milwaukee Library, December 2008, VHS 0589.

BIBLIOGRAPHY

Mazza, Theodore. Papers. Milwaukee County Historical Society, Milwaukee, WI.
Milwaukee Journal, December 1926–November 1966.
Milwaukee Sentinel, 1903.
Pizzino, Peter, and Tom Montag. *Peter's Story: Growing up in Milwaukee's Third Ward during the 1920s & 1930s.* Fairwater, WI: Midwestern Writers Publishing House Books, 2007.
"Resconto Finanziario Della Chiesa," Madonna Di Pompompei Per'L Anno 1934, Milwaukee Archdiocese Archives, Milwaukee, WI.
Stern, Erich C. Papers, 1868–1967. University of Wisconsin–Milwaukee Archives, Milwaukee, WI.
Tagliavia, Salvatore. Essay, circa 1945. Milwaukee Collection 72. University of Wisconsin-Milwaukee Archives, Milwaukee, WI.
Tanzilo, Robert. Papers. Immigration History Research Center, University of Minnesota, Minneapolis, MN.
"Wisconsin Women during World War II Oral History Project Interviews, 1992–94." Wisconsin Historical Society Archives.
Zignego, Michele. Interview with author, January 2009.

SECONDARY SOURCES

Catapano, Peter. "Rise of the Nation-State, 1850–1870." Personal website, December 16, 2008. http://websupport1.citytech.cuny.edu/Faculty/pcatapano/lectures_wc2/map-18-02-p764.jpg. Accessed August 30, 2009.
Choate, Mark I. *Emigrant Nation: The Making of Italy Abroad.* Cambridge, MA: Harvard University Press, 2008.
Cinel, Dino. *The National Integration of Italian Return Migration, 1870–1929.* New York: Cambridge University Press, 1991.
Cochrane, Willian, and Richard Turton, ed. "Italian Unification Map (1850–1870)." *The Philatelic Database*, February 28, 2009. http://www.philatelicdatabase.com/maps/italian-unification-map-18501870/. Accessed August 30, 2009.
Davis, John A., ed. *Italy in the Nineteenth Century.* New York: Oxford University Press, 2000.
Gabaccia, Donna R. *From the Other Side: Women, Gender & Immigrant Life in the U.S. 1820–1990.* Bloomington: Indiana University Press, 1994.

BIBLIOGRAPHY

———. *From Sicily to Elizabeth Street: Housing and Social Change Among Italian Immigrants 1880–1930*. Albany: State University of New York Press, 1984.

———. *Italy's Many Diasporas*. London: University College London Press, 2000.

Goldfield, David. *The American Journey: A History of the United States*, vol. 1, 4th ed. Upper Saddle River, NJ: Pearson Education, 2007.

Greene, Victor. "Dealing With Diversity: Milwaukee's Multiethnic Festivals and Urban Identity, 1840–1940." *Journal of Urban History* 31 (September 2005): 820–49.

Guglielmo, Thomas. *White on Arrival: Italians, Race, Color, and Power in Chicago, 1890–1945*. New York: Oxford University Press, 2003.

"Italy Overview: Maps." *EUGRIS (European Information System Soil and Groundwater): Portal for Soil and Water Management in Europe*. Accessed August 30, 2009. http://www.eugris.info/furtherDescription.asp?GlossaryID=111&ResourceTypes=True&eugrisid=550&Category=Country_Digests&Title=Italy%20overview&showform=&ContentID=3&CountryID=8&ResourceTypes-&DocID=A&Tools=Further%20Description.

National Italian American Foundation. "Italian-American Contributions." *Italian-Americans in U.S. Military History*. Accessed February 25, 2009. http://www.niaf.org/research/contribution.asp#mil. The Italian Community Center. Milwaukee, WI.

Noether, Emiliana. "The Silent Half: Before the First World War." In *The Italian Immigrant Woman in North America*, edited by Betty Caroli. Toronto: The Multicultural History Society of Ontario, 1978.

Vecchio, C. Diane. *Merchants, Midwives, and Laboring Women: Italian Migrants in Urban America*. Chicago: University of Illinois Press, 2006.

Wolfensberger, Don. "Woodrow Wilson, Congress and Anti-Immigrant Sentiment in America an Introductory Essay." Woodrow Wilson International Center for Scholars, 11–12. Accessed December 5, 2008. http://www.wilsoncenter.org/events/docs/immigration-essayintro.pdf.

Woodall, Conrad. "The Italian Massacre at Walsenburg, Colorado, 1895." In *Italian Ethnics: Their Languages, Literature and Lives: Proceedings of the 20th Annual Conference of the American Italian Historical Chicago Association Chicago, Illinois November 11–13, 1987*. Staten Island, NY: The American Historical Association, 1990.

Zamagni, Vera. *The Economic History of Italy, 1860–1990*. Oxford: Clarendon Press, 1993.

BIBLIOGRAPHY

Secondary Sources on Milwaukee

Andreozzi, John. "Contadini and Pescatori in Milwaukee: Assimilation and Voluntary Associations." Master's thesis, University of Wisconsin–Milwaukee, 1974.

Avella, Steven M. *In the Richness of the Earth: A History of the Archdiocese of Milwaukee 1843–1958*. Milwaukee, WI: Marquette University Press & the Archdiocese of Milwaukee, 2002.

Carini, Mario. *Milwaukee's Italians: The Early Years*. Milwaukee, WI: The Italian Community Center of Milwaukee, 1999.

City of Milwaukee Directories.

Curtiss-Wedge, Franklyn. *History of Goodhue County, Minnesota*. Chicago: H.C. Cooper Jr. & Co., 1909.

The Giuseppe Garibaldi Society. Milwaukee, WI.

Gurda, John. "The Church and Neighborhood." In *Milwaukee Catholicism: Essays on Church and Community*. Edited by Steven M. Avella. Milwaukee, WI: Knights of Columbus, 1991.

———. *The Making of Milwaukee*. Brookfield, WI: Burton & Mayer, Inc., Third Edition, 2006.

Hemman, Thomas. "In Memoriam." *Italian Times* 30, no. 7, January 2009.

Milwaukee County Historical Society.

Meloni, Alberto. "Italy Invades the Bloody Third: The Early History of Milwaukee's Italians." *Milwaukee History* 10 (Summer 1987).

Passante, Anna. "Remembering Bay View's Little Italy." *Bay View Compass: The South Shore Bellwether* 4 no. 7, July 2007.

Simonsen, Judith. "The Third Ward: Symbol of Ethnic Identity." *Milwaukee History* 10 (Summer 1987).

Tanzilo, Robert. "Politics, Protest and Proselytization: A Struggle Among Italian-Americans in 1917 Milwaukee." Unpublished book, 2007.

Zignego Co. Inc.

About the Author

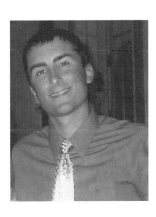

Anthony M. Zignego is a Milwaukee-born historian who has earned a BA and an MA in history from the University of Wisconsin–Milwaukee. He specializes in nineteenth- and twentieth-century United States immigration and urban history, and this is his first book.

Zignego has taught college courses on United States and European history. He speaks Spanish, Italian and English. He is currently employed by Zignego Co., Inc., in Waukesha, Wisconsin.

Visit us at
www.historypress.net